The Power of
Positive Words

Dr Theo Wolmarans

Published by: Theo & Beverley Christian Enterprises
Address: P.O. Box 8141, Bonaero Park, 1622, South Africa
Tel: +27 11 230 9312
Email address book orders only: TheoandBev@cfcsa.co.za

Cover Design:
Layout & Typesetting: The Icon Agency, Centurion, South Africa
Printed and bound by Interpak Books, Pietermaritzburg, South Africa

ISBN: 978-0-620-44637-2

Dedication

To my amazing wife Beverley.

God knew what He needed when He gave you to me. You inspired me to write my books — you have never let it rest until I got it done — thank you. You are the love of my life and I thank you for all the support and encouragement you have given me through the years.

I love you with all my heart.

Theo

Contents

Acknowledgements

To my Saviour and Lord Jesus Christ. Through all eternity I'll have the privilege of thanking You for the wonderful salvation You gave so much for me to receive. I deeply appreciate how much you've honoured me by calling me to serve You in the ministry. Thank you for an amazing life here on earth - there is nothing else that can compare to the joy and fulfilment of working for My King.

To Pastor George and Heloise Dillman. I know you made many large personal sacrifices in order to establish such a great successful church in Durban North. You lived lives of integrity, character and Godly holiness throughout your 50 years of full time ministry. Thank you for personally leading me to the Lord Jesus Christ.

To Kenneth E. Hagin. Like Paul the Apostle sat at the feet of Gamaliel, I've sat at your feet. You have demonstrated a life of integrity, passion and hunger for more of God. My entire Christian foundation was gained by endlessly studying your tapes and books. I will be eternally grateful for your legacy.

To Dr. Yonggi Cho. Thank you for being my pastor for more than 20 years.

I would also like to honor E. W. Kenyon, Watchman Nee and K. J. Conner for their influence in my life. I have learned much from studying their teachings through the years.

To my family. Thank you for your support and encouragement through the years. I'm very proud of my daughters and sons-in-law, and all my grandchildren, you mean the world to me.

To my editors Cori Smelker and Ps. Annette Myers. Cori, thank you for going the extra mile and your amazing work. Annette, thank you for a lifetime of dedication to Bev and me, and for your help to make this book happen.

To Andrew Williams. Thank you for designing the cover of my book. I think it's great and I'm sure everyone else will like it too.

To my friends. Thank you for the many years of wonderful memories.

To pastors, staff, sons and daughters in the faith and all members of Christian Family Church worldwide. It's been a privilege to serve you as unto the Lord, the many years of love and support I have sensed coming from you has been a great encouragement to me many times through the years.

Chapter One

The Importance of Words

It is impossible to live a successful Christian life without understanding the power of positive words. In order to be victorious and face life's challenges, we need to boldly speak the word of God in every circumstance. Speaking positive words is not all there is to being a successful Christian, however, without speaking positive words, one can never be a successful Christian.

As you read this book, you will learn how to release your faith because confessing what the word of God says is putting faith into action. I believe as you read this book, and apply this teaching you will also notice your faith level rise. You will notice unconsciously that you will be doing things and saying things that release faith. So you will see your finances improve, you will see your family relationships improve, you will see your health improve, you will see all circumstances around you line up with the word of God, because you will begin applying faith in every area of your life. In the same way you drive a car automatically, and don't think about it, so you will find yourself applying faith automatically, without thinking about it. These principles work and you will see and enjoy the benefits.

> **Proverbs 18:21 (NKJ)** . . . *death and life are in the power of the tongue.*

"Death and life are in the power of the tongue." God could have said that death and life are in His hands, but He said death and life are in the power of **our** tongue. He adds, *"**therefore choose life**."* In other words, don't release death into our circumstances, release life. This is the way we use faith, and faith is essential in this life. Without faith we cannot succeed in life.

- We cannot please God without faith, according to **Hebrews 11:6**.
- We cannot live a healthy life without faith.
- We cannot prosper without faith.
- We cannot be saved without faith.
- We cannot go to heaven without faith.
- We cannot receive grace without faith.

I have been asked whether I am taking this too far because grace is God's gift, a gift of His unmerited favor. But the Bible says we are '**saved by grace through faith**' (**Ephesians 2:8**). The reason we received the grace of salvation in the first place is because we believe. This grace is available to everyone, but some people choose not to believe in the grace given, therefore they haven't received the grace of salvation.

> Grace comes by faith. The more faith I have, the
> more grace works in my life.

> **Hebrews 11:6 (NKJ)** *Without faith it is impossible
> to receive anything from the Lord.*

Some people think God will help them if they get desperate. But the Bible says without faith it is impossible to receive anything from God, no matter how desperate we are.

> **Romans 14:23 (NKJ)** *What is not of faith is sin.*

I did not write that, so don't think I am strange. If we try and solve all our problems in our own strength, not trusting God to assist, then we enter a realm of presumption and sin, depending on the flesh. We become like **un**circumcised people who depend on the flesh. We are not to trust in the flesh but trust in the Lord with all our heart.

Other people think money will solve all their problems. *"If only I had more money then everything would be fine,"* they say. Money does solve many problems, and money is a great blessing of the Lord, but it can never be compared with the greatness and power and ability of God. There are some things that money can't buy. When the doctor backs off from your bed and says, *"I'm sorry there's nothing we can do for you, you will be dead in 6 months,"* all the money in the world can't fix that. If you're driving down the freeway and a Mack truck crashes into your car, money can't solve that problem. I've seen rich people have divorce in their home and their kids scatter. Money didn't solve their problems.

Say this, *"There are some things money can't solve, and I need to have my priorities right. God first, then all His blessings."*

God's protection is necessary and essential. According to **Psalm 91**, 'His angels camp around us.' Without His protection all the money in the world will not help us.

> There are some things money can't solve, and I need to have my priorities right. God first, then all His blessings.

Mark 9:23 (KJ) *All things are possible to him that believeth.*

Faith is therefore more important than money because with faith in God, money will come. Money is a blessing of the Lord, but we need to have our priorities right. To focus on the gift (money) instead of the giver (God) would be wrong.

When we make bold positive confessions, and **act** in line with them, we put our faith into action. Another way to look at it is — we release our faith when we make bold positive confessions of what God can do and will do in our life and then **act** in line with them.

> Only when I boldly confess, then and then only, do
> I possess.

I could have titled this book, '**The Power Of Negative Words**.' Negative words have just as much power as positive words — they will also bring results, bad ones. The Bible says that death and life are in the power of the tongue. That means the tongue can produce negative things in our life like death, destruction, failure, sickness, poverty, and discouragement.

On the positive side our tongue can produce health, joy, peace, prosperity, success and a Godly blessed family with Godly blessed obedient children. We will also become successful soul winners when we use our faith.

> Speaking positively is not all there is to being a
> successful Christian.
> However, without speaking positively I can never be
> a successful Christian.

We can become successful soul winners if we use our faith.

Say this, *"I am a soul winner. God brings folks to me that I can influence toward the gospel."*

We can follow God's plan and fulfill God's destiny for our lives by using our faith and speaking correctly. God has a purpose for bringing us to the earth at this time. This is a crucial time in the history of the church and God has a plan, a purpose, and a destiny for our lives. I believe you can fulfill that plan.

Say this, *"God has a plan for my life and I believe I know what that plan is and I am obedient to that plan."* We can also say it this way, *"I receive God's guidance every day according to* **Colossians 1:9**, *and He orders my steps according to* **Psalm 37:23**.*"* We can say the same thing in various ways, but when we speak it out, and believe it in our hearts, that is what God will do for us. If we keep saying it, faith will rise and we will walk in the fulfillment of it.

In order to activate our faith, it is essential that we analyze our words. Our words are like seeds and every word we speak is a seed planted. Soon enough it will germinate and bear its fruit. We will then either enjoy the fruit or be harassed by the fruit of our words. We can plant good seeds or we can plant weeds with our words. We can plant victories and happiness in our life by what we say, or we can plant problems in our life by what we say. Our words will produce joy or failure because death and life are in the power of the tongue.

Say this, *"God cannot do more for me than my words of faith allow Him to do, because God will not do anything for us if there is no faith involved."*

> God cannot do more for me than my words of faith allow Him to do, because He will not act if there's no faith involved.

James 1:6 (NKJ) *But let him ask in faith...*
⁷ For let not that man suppose that (without faith) he will receive anything from the Lord;

Say this, *"All I am today is a culmination of the words I have spoken in the past."*

We can therefore see that all we are today is a culmination of the words we have spoken in the past. If we are not satisfied with our life it is not the problems of life that have made us this way, it is the words we **have failed to speak** to our problems. It is not the giants of life that defeat us. David proved that. The entire army of Israel shivered in their boots and their knees had fellowship when Goliath came out. But David said, *"This day the Lord will give you into my hands."* It was those words that slew Goliath, not his sling and the stone. When he spoke those words, God took the sling and slew Goliath.

> If I speak positively into my circumstances, God will
> anoint my abilities.
> He will anoint my resources.

If we speak positively into our circumstances, God will anoint our abilities. He'll anoint our resources. These words are extremely important. God cannot do things for us; God cannot move on our behalf, even though He desires to, unless we give Him the opportunity. The Bible says about the children of Israel that the word of God did not profit them because it was not mixed with faith:

> **Hebrews 4:2 (NKJ)** ... *but the word which they heard did not profit them, not being mixed with faith in those who heard it.*

How were the children of Israel supposed to mix the word of God with faith? They could have said, *"God said so-and-so... I believe that that is for me. I have it now, praise God it is mine."* If they had done that, they would have mixed faith with God's word and what they said would have been theirs. **When we do this, we mix faith with God's word and then it becomes ours.** You say, *"Well that's great Pastor Theo, but the church is not doing that."*

The Bible says:

> **James 2:20 (NKJ)** *Faith without works is dead.*

It could have been written like this, *"By **not** agreeing with the word of God, and declaring what God says, and acting like it is true, faith won't work."* We can have all the faith in the world, but if we don't apply it, it is the same as not having any faith. If we have the faith and don't use it, we are like a person who gets attacked at night and who has a weapon to defend themself but doesn't use it. They might as well not have one.

When a problem comes our way, are we going to say, *"what are we going do now Pastor Theo, what are we going to do now?"* This is what we are going to do. We are just going to act like the Bible is true! Let's stay calm and just act like the Bible is true. You might do it with your knees shaking, having fellowship, that's fine. Just do it! The Lord is going to rescue us. He is not going to let us fail.

Now Christians who understand the subject of the power of positive words are very careful not to make any negative statements. You hear folks in a conversation who have heard teaching like this. Somebody says something negative and they say, *"You know, I wouldn't say that, that's negative."* They are right. We are very careful not to say anything negative over our families, our businesses, our finances, our health, our circumstances and that's good. But you know where we fail? We fail by not making positive statements. **We neglect to say something positive in a negative situation.**

It's like preparing a beautiful garden at home. We want to plant carrots in it, so we dig it out, make it nice; we get our seeds and put them down on the side. We dig up all the weeds and say to ourselves, *"I'm not going to let any weeds get into my garden."* We put a little fence around it and won't let anyone go there. We won't let any wind blow any bad seeds in and make sure there are no weeds around. We do everything possible to keep every negative thing out. A year later we come back, look at our garden and wonder why there are no carrots. Because we never planted any carrots!

And that's how folks look over their life. They think, *"I've been serving God all these years. I don't have any serious problems but I don't have the blessings I see so many others have."* Some Christians are like the rich obedient son, who said, *"Father all these years I've served you, and you never gave me even a skinny goat, but you gave this backslidden son who came home the fattened lamb."* These people serve God and never put their word out, never say what God will do, therefore they settle for second best in life. They won't be fulfilling God's plan and destiny like that.

If we start confessing, *"I **am** fulfilling God's plan for my life,"* Guess what? We will start walking in the will of God. God will bring us into His plan and all the resources we need to fulfill it will come our way. We'll find ourselves blessed beyond measure. All things are possible to him that believeth. And God is not limited. Let us not miss the opportunity of speaking positively in every situation.

I know people who've actually died with sickness and they have had a heart full of faith to be healed, but they didn't use it. I've been at their bedside and said, *"I know you believe, but let's use our faith, this is how we do it."* People who die with a heart full of faith, die for one of two reasons. Either they don't know how to use the faith they have, or secondly, they know how to use it, but don't.

Remember, faith comes by hearing and hearing. It is not by struggling and struggling or stressing and stressing. By reading the Bible your faith will rise. You will know it because the first thing that faith brings into your heart is peace and joy.

The Bible says:

> **Hebrews 4:3 (NKJ)** *For we who have believed do enter that rest,*

The first thing that faith brings is rest and peace into your heart. You just know that everything is fine. You might be standing in the eye of the storm, but you will have a smile on your face.

> **Proverbs 6:2 (NKJ)** *You are snared by the words of your mouth; you are taken by the words of your mouth.*

A snare is a trap that a poacher uses to catch animals out in the bush. He knows he's not supposed to, but he hides a trap out in the bush and the animals unsuspectingly walk into it and get caught. God says, 'Our words are like a snare to us.' Those are negative words obviously. In other words, our words hold us in invisible chains. Our words hold us prisoner and captive. Our words create circumstances, and the circumstances control us completely because of our words. God is powerless to move in those circumstances. We speak what we see. We declare our problem, and talk about our problem. Our problem gets bigger when we do. Our problem stands like a mountain before us. A molehill turns into a mountain because of our words. Instead of speaking negatively about our problems, we can say this, *"If I speak about the mountain it will grow. If I speak to the mountain, it will go."*

If I speak about the mountain it will grow.
If I speak to the mountain, it will go.

The Bible says, *"You are snared with the words of your mouth."* It is not the problems of life that are our problem. The biggest problem we have is found one inch below our nose!

Satan understands the power of positive words; he also understands the power of negative confession. He has tried to program the unsaved world to speak negatively all the time. This has happened to me several times and I am sure you have experienced the same thing. I phone a company to speak to somebody, and when the receptionist or the secretary answer, I will ask to speak to Fred Bloggs and they say, *"I'm afraid he's not in."* I reply, *"Well, don't be afraid, he'll come back. There's no need to be in fear over that."* We know they are not afraid, but the point is, people confess their fears without even realizing it. They are programmed to speak negatively.

We've all met people who talk about their fears all the time and say, 'I'm afraid of this, I'm afraid of that. I'm afraid I can't come, I'm afraid I should have come. I'm afraid that you didn't come.' They talk about everything they're afraid of until they get to a place where they walk in absolute fear.

> **Mark 11:12 (NKJ)** *The next day when they had come out from Bethany, Jesus was hungry.*

If you have been to Israel, you know that Bethany is on the east side of Jerusalem, about two miles away. When people walked from Bethany to Jerusalem they went over the Mount of Olives, down the other side, through the Kidron Valley and up into Jerusalem. Jesus walked from Bethany to Jerusalem and stopped on the Mount of Olives, in the Garden of Gethsemane, a place where He had spent many hours in prayer. He saw a fig tree that had leaves on it. At that time of year, if a fig tree had leaves on it, it would also have figs. So He thought there should be figs on the fig tree.

> [13] *And seeing from afar a fig tree having leaves He went to see if perhaps He would find something on it. When he came to it, He found nothing but leaves.*

14 In response Jesus said to it, "Let no one eat fruit from you ever again." And His disciples heard it.

He could not have whispered that statement otherwise His disciples would not have heard it; neither did He think it. He must have said it loudly enough that all of the disciples could hear it.

> It's not enough to think our confessions.
> We have to say them.

In **Mark 5** the woman with the issue of blood was making her way to Jesus when she said, *"If I can just touch the hem of His garment I shall be made well."*

She never thought that. She said it over and over, *"If I can get there I* **shall** *be made well, I* **shall** *be made well."*

Mark 11:15 (NKJ) *So they came to Jerusalem...*
19 when evening had come He went out of the city.

Jesus returned to Bethany where He had started out that morning. He was probably staying at Lazarus' house, His friend whom He raised from the dead on the fourth day. The next morning He made His way from Lazarus' house in Bethany back to Jerusalem.

> **Mark 11:20 (NKJ)** *Now in the morning, as they passed by, they saw the fig tree dried up from the roots.*
>
> *²¹ And Peter, remembering, said to Him, "Rabbi look! The fig tree which You cursed (yesterday) has withered away."*

Now Peter said that Jesus **cursed** the fig tree, when all He said to the tree was, *"Let no man eat fruit from you again."* Jesus did not say, *"Peter, don't accuse Me of cursing this tree. I just spoke to the tree."* Jesus did not defend Himself, instead He agreed. Jesus cursed the tree intentionally because it was a non-productive tree. It was supposed to have been bearing fruit and it wasn't. We can see this great truth from Peter's statement, *"Anything negative I ever say is a curse according to the Bible."*

Let's imagine somebody has a 4-year old, and in his son's presence, he says to his friends, *"My wife and I barely made it through school. I guess little Johnny is as dumb as we are, maybe dumber. He'll never make it through school. I pity him when he goes to school."* That parent might as well take little Johnny down to the witch doctor and say, *"Mr. Witch Doctor curse my son with as much stupidity as you can muster."*

Alternatively, they say, *"My wife and I never communicate. We just have a bad relationship."* Why not say, *"My wife and I have a great relationship"*? Perhaps they confess, *"My kids are so unruly, I don't know how I'm going to manage them."* Why not say, *"Praise God I have obedient kids,"* and give God a chance to work with the kids, or perhaps God will teach **you** how manage them, if that's the cause of the problem.

Anything negative I ever say is a curse according to the Bible.

When we say, *"My kids are so unruly and lawless. They never listen to anything I say,"* you just opened a door for the devil to make them worse. We're cursing our children, cursing our circumstances, cursing our life. It doesn't happen the first time we say it but if we keep saying it, it won't be long before we will believe those words. If we keep saying it, soon enough we're going to believe those words. The moment we believe them and say them again, we release creative force. We release the ability of God, or the ability of the devil.

> **Mark 11:22 (NKJ)** *So Jesus answered and said to them, "Have faith in God."*

Peter had just pointed out that Jesus spoke to the tree and it died. Now the Lord says to disciples, *"I want you to have faith in God."* The Worrell translation says it this way:

> **Mark 11:22 (Worrell)** *and Jesus answering said to them, "Have the faith of God."*

Have the faith **of** God. Some translations have this written in the margin. '**Have the God kind of faith**.' Jesus was telling the disciples as they looked at the fig tree, "**have the God kind of faith**." In other words, Jesus is saying, '**You can use the God kind of faith** in **your** life the way I used the God kind of faith on this fig tree. You can use the same kind of faith that I exercised when I spoke to the fig tree.' He goes on to explain how the God kind of faith works in the next verse.

²³ *"For assuredly I say to you…"*

The Lord says, *"**assuredly**"*. He could have said, *"I say it to you"*, but He didn't. He said, *"For **assuredly** I say to you."* That sounds far more important. He wants to make us understand that this is the way it is and there is no other way. This will **definitely** work.

²³ *"For assuredly I say to you, <u>whoever</u> says…"*

Surely the Lord meant to say, 'Whichever Christian says…' No! I know, surely the Lord meant to say, 'Whichever Godly person says…' No! He says, 'Whoever…' That means He is talking to us — to you and me — now.'

²³ *…<u>Whoever</u> says to this mountain…*

He's probably standing on the Mount of Olives, between Bethany and Jerusalem.

> [23] *"Assuredly I say to you, whoever says to this*
> *mountain be removed and be cast into the sea."*

Look at those words, *"Be removed and be cast into the sea..."* That is a total of eight words. So, **whoever** says these eight words "**and**,

> [23] *...does not doubt in his heart, but believes that*
> *those things he says will be done, he will have*
> *whatever he says."*

There is no doubt allowed. But surely the Lord meant to say, *"He will have **some** of the things he says."* But that's not what it says, is it? He shall have what? '**Whatever** he says.' Does that mean only good things? Or does that include bad things? Does that include everything?

What is '**whatever**' in the Greek? It is whatever. Why? Because that's what '**whatever**' means. That means whatever we've been saying about our finances is what we have today. **Or the positive things we neglected to say about our finances, is what we don't have today.** That means whatever we've been saying about our physical condition is what we have today. Whatever we've been saying about our marriage and our job is what we have today.

If we come home from work and say to our spouse, *"My boss doesn't like me, honey. I went to work today and he didn't talk to me."*
Your spouse may say, *"Do you think he might have just been pensive and thinking about something else?"*

But you say, *"I told you, he doesn't like me. I walked right by him and he didn't even notice me."*

A year later he fires you, and you come home and say, *"You see, I told you so. I knew it was going to happen."*

Now you think you are a prophet! In the meantime you caused it. You are not a prophet. It is a mystery to you. You say, *"I don't know how it worked, but it happened and he fired me. I knew it all the time."*

People ask me, *"Pastor Theo, how come there are folks out there that don't believe in Jesus, they don't serve Jesus, but they're rich. Look at Donald Trump and so many others like him. How come they're rich and they aren't Bible-practicing Christians? Why do I have to use this faith stuff and they don't?"*

Here is the news. They do! It works for **whoever** says. I guarantee, if you were to interview Donald Trump, he would not say, *"I'm poor, I don't know how I ever made it, and I don't know how I'm going to make it the next week. Pray for me because I'm in trouble and I know I will never get through this. You know, I've got the Apprentice coming up and I just don't know how that's going to work. You all pray for me now. Perhaps it'll be okay. Who knows? I'm going to try and buy this building but they probably won't accept my offer."* No, not a chance in a million! If you talk to Donald Trump he will tell you how many millions he's made, and how many more he's going to make. He is one of the most successful men in the world. He's a multi-billionaire and he's going to make more billions.

A lady recently told me that a friend of hers was buying a tie in a clothing store in Donald Trump's building and Donald walked in as her friend was trying on the tie. Donald said, *"If you buy that tie, it will make you a billionaire."* He continued, *"I didn't say millions, anybody can make millions, I said billionaire."* And he walked out. I doubt that tie is going to make the man into a billionaire but the point is, Donald thinks big in everything he does. There's not an ounce of negativity in his whole body. No wonder he's successful in finances. But remember, money has its place. Faith is more important than finances, because faith can get you everything you need. Finances can't.

> **Romans 4:17 (NKJ)** *God calls those things which do not exist as though they did;*

What does that mean? Paul is talking about Abraham right here in Romans. Now let's look at the scripture Paul was referring to.

> **Genesis 17:5 (NKJ)** *No longer shall your name be called Abram, but your name shall be Abraham; for I have made you a father of many nations.*

The name Abraham in the Hebrew language means, 'father of many nations.' So when Abraham said, *"Hello, my name is Abraham,"* the Hebrew person he spoke to heard, *"my name is 'father of many nations,'"* because that is what his name means in Hebrew. So God changed his name and yet Isaac was still not born. In verse 21, God says to Abraham:

> ²¹ *But My covenant I will establish with Isaac, whom Sarah shall bear to you at this set time next year.*

God changed his name to Abraham before Isaac was born. Let us go back and look at verse 5. Is that **past** tense, **future** tense or **present** tense? When God said, *"Abraham I* **have** *made you the father of many nations,"* is that future — I'm **going** to do it. I plan to do it. Get ready for it? Or was that already a done deal? It would either be present tense or past tense. I believe it qualifies for both. So God calls those things that be not as though they were. That's why God said in:

> **1 Peter 2:24 (NKJ)** *By whose stripes you* **were** *healed.*

He said, 2000 years ago you were healed. This is **past** tense. That's why God wrote in **Isaiah 53:5**, *"by whose stripes we* **are** *healed,"* before Jesus came to the earth. That's why the Bible says Christ is the lamb from the foundation of the world (**Revelation 13:8**).

God calls those things that be not as though they were. In other words, when God says it is so, it becomes so. When God says it is so that it settles it, nothing can alter that. When God says something about us, it is so. The minute we say what God says we start entering **into** the experience of it. So, we must call those things that be not as though they were. We must say, *"By Jesus' stripes I* **am** *healed,"* even if we have pain in our body.

People have said, *"Pastor Theo I'm not going to do that, that would be lying. I'm not going to say it is so when it is not so because I don't want to lie."* Well family, if God says it and He's not lying, it is okay for us to do so too, if there's faith involved. Now to tell a lie is different. We are not talking about that. I'm not saying it is okay to lie. But if you are using your faith and saying, *"Praise God I'm prospering,"* when you are as poor as a church mouse, you are using faith, and that's not a lie.

> The minute we say what God says we start entering into the experience of it.

Let's for example say somebody weighs 160 lbs and they want to lose 10 lbs. Would this be a good confession? *"Praise God I have 10 lbs to lose."* Would it work for them? No! They will always have 10 lbs to lose because they say, *"I have 10 lbs to lose."* When the rapture comes they'll go up with 10 lbs to lose. If you weigh 160 lbs and you want to weigh 150lbs, then say, *"Praise God I believe I weigh 150 lbs."* You might say, *"But I've been saying that for a whole month and nothing's changed."* Keep saying it because your faith is rising and soon you're going to believe it, and guess what? God will bring whatever it is you need, either a change in diet, a new diet, or the correct exercise.

Joel 3:10 (NKJ) *Let the weak say, I am strong.*

God wanted to prepare Israel for war but they were just farmers at that time. God said, *"I want you to take your pruning hooks, and beat them into swords. Beat your plowshares into shields. Get ready for war, and then, farmers, I want you who are weak to say,* **1 am strong**.*"* He could have said, *"Get up and start saying, 'I* **hope** *to be strong, I'm* **going to be** *strong or I'm* **working out** *to be strong.'"* No. He said, *"Say I am strong."* When they said it, God made them strong.

That's why God came to Gideon and said, *"Gideon, mighty man of valor."* Gideon turned around and said. *"Who me?"* He added, *"Our tribe is the weakest of the twelve tribes. And our clan is the weakest in our tribe. And our family is the weakest in our clan. And I'm just the ding-a-ling of my family, the worst of the whole bunch. And you call me a mighty man of valor?"* In other words, *"Dear God! I think you have the wrong man!"* God knew who the weakest man in all of Israel was. He came to Gideon purposely and said, *"I'm on your side. Therefore you are a mighty man of valor."*

If God is with us we are more than a conqueror. It is like little kids getting in a fight and they're bold as a lion because their big brothers are there. When big brothers are not there, they're quiet. We can be as bold as a lion because our big brother is with us. His name is Jesus! We can say with confidence, *"I am strong. I am rich. I am healthy. I solve every problem with God's wisdom, God's ability, and God's resources. I know what to do in every circumstance. God guides me, and He blesses me. My family is in unity. My family serves God. We love God together. All my family is saved. I am a soul winner."*

- "I'm blessed!
- I'm highly favored.
- I am favored by God.
- I am favored by man.
- Everybody wants to bless me.
- Everybody wants to do things for me.
- Wherever I go people trip over themselves to help me.
- I get put to the front of the line.
- Money comes to me from all directions because I'm highly favored. I'm blessed and highly favored.
- I'm blessed in the city, blessed in the field.
- I am blessed coming in. I am blessed going out.
- I am blessed by God. Thank you Jesus.
- All these blessings are mine so I can be a greater blessing to others. So I can influence more people to Christ."

Chapter Two

Using Our Faith

We must understand how important it is to be able to use our faith, because if we don't, God can never help us, no matter how serious or tragic our circumstances may be.

> **James 1:7 (NKJ)** *Without faith it is impossible to receive anything from the Lord.*

> **Romans 12:1 (NKJ)** *I beseech you therefore, brethren, by the mercies of God, that you present your bodies a living sacrifice, holy, acceptable to God, which is your reasonable service.*
>
> *² And do not be conformed to this world, but be transformed by the renewing of your mind, that you may prove what is that good and acceptable and perfect will of God.*

In order to know **either** the **good**, or the **acceptable**, or the **perfect** will of God, we need to have our mind renewed to the word. We need to know what God thinks about certain things, otherwise how can we know what God's will is in our circumstances?

By reading this book we are going to have our minds renewed. When we go out into the marketplace, or to work, or go to school and educate ourselves, we rub shoulders with people out in the world who speak doubt, unbelief, fear, and talk about their problems. There are many voices. These things drain us of our faith. That's why we need to come to church and have our mind washed with the word. The Bible talks about the washing of the water by the word (**Ephesians 5:26**). We must have our mind washed with the word, so we can understand the good and perfect will of God and walk in it.

When you drive your car, you can have a conversation with someone at the same time. You're not even really thinking about the things you do while driving. Obviously you are concentrating on where you are going, but you can drive automatically because it's natural. You don't have to concentrate on putting your foot on the brake. You do that when it's necessary without thinking about it. After hearing the word and having our brains washed, having our mind renewed as to how faith works, and having our hearts filled with the word of God, we'll find that we'll be using faith as unconsciously as we drive a car.

By using our faith, unconsciously we'll be speaking to our finances, speaking to our family situations, speaking to our spiritual life, speaking to our physical bodies and we will find releasing faith in these areas will bring prosperity and will bring improvement in our health, in our relationships, and in our peace, love, joy and everything else that God has provided for us in this life. We will see things improve without stress, and without having to think about it, because our heart and mind are being renewed to a walk of faith

Say this, *"It is important for me to have my mind and heart renewed and refreshed in my faith walk. For without faith I cannot receive anything from the Lord."*

> **Mark 4:13 (NKJ)** *And He said to them, "Do you not understand this parable? How then will you understand all the parables?"*

In other words, the Lord Jesus is saying that the particular parable we are about to read, or what He is about to say, is extremely important. It is the basis, the foundation, and the principle for all parables. If we don't understand this parable we will not be able to understand any other parable.

Say this, *"This is important. What I am about to hear I need to understand."*

14 The sower sows the word.

A farmer would sow corn out on his farm, or some other seed and that would produce a harvest. The Lord Jesus said here in **Mark 4:14** that the word is going to be sown. You might say — speaking God's word is a farming experience. Right now, I would be the sower. If you were witnessing to somebody you would be the sower. But today I'm the sower, the word is the seed and you are the soil. Your heart is the soil, and the seed, which is the word, is going to go into your heart. Now, whatever seed is sown, if you allow it to, will germinate in your heart and produce a harvest.

> *1 Peter 1:23 (NKJ) (you) have been born again,* **not of corruptible seed but incorruptible, through the word of God** *which lives and abides forever.*

The Bible tells us **the word of God is incorruptible seed**. For example, if I say, according to **Luke 6:38**, *"I have given, therefore it is given unto me good measure, pressed down, shaken together and running over."* When I say that, I am planting a financial faith seed, and it will produce a financial harvest for me.

According to **1 Peter 2:24**, 'By Jesus stripes I was healed,' is a healing seed. If I sow that seed into my heart by saying it, it will produce a health harvest.

All seed produces after its kind. Carrot seed produces carrots. Mango seed produces mangoes, dog seed produces dogs, and human seed produces humans. God has seed, and His seed is the word.

All seed produces after its kind.

> **1 Peter 1:23 (NKJ)** ...*not of corruptible **seed** but incorruptible, through the **word of God** which lives and abides forever,*

That means the word carries God's life in it, just like human seed carries human life in it. God's seed carries His life in it. When an unsaved person, hearing the word of God preached, receives the word of God and accepts it, he gets born again. In other words, the life of God enters that person's heart, and now he's alive with the life of God in him. God's life entered into his heart through the spoken word. Christ is alive in that man. How? By receiving the seed that carried the life.

Jesus said in:

> **John 6:63 (NKJ)** *The **words** that I speak to you are **spirit**, and they are **life**.*

So every word of God carries life and every seed will produce after its own kind. In every seed is the ability to produce its own harvest.

In every seed is the ability to produce its own harvest.

In the following parable, we will notice six different kinds of soil, three categories that are bad and three that are good.

29

There is **wayside** soil, **thorny** soil, **stony** ground, and **good** ground that produces 30, 60, and 100-fold return. As we go through this parable, let us carefully analyze this to see where we are. Which category do we fit into? Are we the good soil? Or do we occasionally drift into one of the categories of the bad soil?

> **Mark 4:14 (NKJ)** *The sower sows the word.*
> ¹⁵ *And these are the ones by the **wayside** where the word is sown. When they hear, Satan comes immediately and takes away the word that was sown in their hearts.*

As people journeyed from one place to another in those times, out in the countryside, they would create a pathway, called the **wayside**. If seed fell on the wayside it would obviously not germinate and bear a harvest as it would be trampled down. The ground was very hard, thin and crusted. The Lord Jesus said this group of people is like **wayside soil** because they **hear the word** and Satan comes **immediately** and **steals the word** that was sown in their hearts. So, if the word is sown into a heart now — how long would it take the devil to take it out of the heart if he did it immediately? How much time lapses between the time that the word **is received**, and the time that the word is **taken**? If the word of God is taken immediately, how long does it take before the word is taken out of the heart? Right now while you are reading? Is that what it means? You mean some people are going to be hearing and not perceiving? Some people are not going to comprehend? Is that what that means? It means some people are listening (or reading) but they are not taking it in. The word of God says Satan comes immediately and takes away the word that was sown in their hearts. Who did it? Who makes us lose our concentration? Satan. Why? He's after the word. Keep that in mind.

Let's go over to Luke and look at his account of this parable. Mark and Luke both write about it, and Luke will shed more light on the subject. We'll get additional information to help us understand a little more clearly what the Lord is talking about.

> **Luke 8:11 (NKJ)** *Now the parable is this:* **The seed is the word of God.**

We can see from this that God's word is seed. At this point, and at this verse, take your pen and write **1 Peter 1:23**. That verse tells us the word of God is incorruptible seed. Then go to **1 Peter 1:23** and write **Luke 8:11** as a cross-reference for the two scriptures. That gives us two scriptures to confirm that God's word is seed. The Bible says, 'out of the mouth of two or three witnesses let every truth be established.'

Jesus said in **John 6:63,** 'my words are spirit and they are life.' You could write the other two scripture references there too, which now gives three witnesses to tell you that the word carries life. You can also write in:

> **John 1:1 (NKJ)** *In the beginning was the Word,*
> *and the Word was with God and the Word was God.*
>
> [14] *And the Word became flesh and dwelt among us,*
> *and we beheld His glory, the glory as of the only*
> *begotten of the Father, full of grace and truth.*

So the Word walked the earth and revealed the written word to people, but they could not perceive it, because they were not born again. Those who are born again have the life of God in them, thus they can understand the scripture. We don't need the Lord to appear in a physical body. But in the beginning was the word, so put your hand on your Bible and say, *"Jesus and the written word are one, and the written word has life in it."* Now, we must understand the power of God's word. Christ stood up on nothing, and said, *"Let light be,"* and the Holy Spirit created the stars and sun at that moment.

> **Genesis 1:26 (NKJ)** *Then God said, Let Us (plural)*
> *make man in Our (plural) image."*

The Father, the Son, and the Holy Spirit were all involved in creation together. The Father gave permission and Christ, the Word, said, *"Light be"*. Then what you see out in space at night began from one focal point and went outwards in all directions. All those stars and lights out in the universe are all a result of one seed, 'light be'. If you could go back in time, everything would go back into those words, 'light be'. God's word hasn't lost any of its power. It's incorruptible; it cannot fail.

The reason we don't see the harvest is because of the soil. The soil determines the harvest. The seed can only produce what the soil allows it to produce. If our faith is not working don't be concerned about the seed. Don't worry about whether God's word can do it. We need to look at the heart. How hungry is the heart for God and His word?

> **Luke 8:11 (NKJ)** *Now the parable is this: The seed is the word of God.*
>
> [12] *Those by the wayside are the ones who hear; then the devil comes and takes away* **the word out of their hearts**, *lest they should believe and be saved.*

Say this, *"The heart is the soil that the seed is planted into in order to bear a harvest."*

So, the seed is the word and the soil is man's heart. Jesus said the seed gets into the heart by the way we hear. That's why Jesus said, *"take heed* **how** *you hear"* (**Mark 4:24**). **How** we hear and **what** we hear is extremely important when it comes to the subject of growing faith. The Bible said we are to fight the good fight of faith. There is a fight to faith. If we want to start using faith to receive something from God there **is** a fight to it. What we want will not fall on us like ripe cherries off a tree. There is a fight to the fight of faith. God could have said, 'Be positive to use your faith.' He could have said, 'Try and use your faith.' But He chose the word fight because there **is** a fight to it. Why? Satan is trying to steal the word, which causes the faith to come — the word carries faith in it. That's why there is a fight

33

to faith. Now where exactly is the fight? What would I be doing if I wanted to enter that fight of faith? What would my action be? Confession is part of it. But 95% of the fight is in the area of meditating on the verse specific to the area you want answers to. For example, for healing you would meditate on **1 Peter 2:24**, *"by Jesus stripes you were healed,"* and then say it out loud over and over.

That's 95% of the fight of faith. Meditating on the verse. Why? Because faith comes by hearing, and hearing, and hearing, the word of God (**Romans 10:17**). Jesus said, *"from the abundance of the heart the mouth speaks."* It is not hard to speak what's in your heart. Just fill your heart and it will do its own speaking. You won't have to worry about doing all the confessions if you will just fill your heart with the promise; the confessions will come out automatically.

Just walk down the street or in the mall and listen to people talking, you'll see what's in their heart because it comes out of the mouth. We have to program our heart. That's where the fight is. Satan is trying to take the word out of the heart, and we are trying to put the word into our heart. That's where the fight is. Keep looking at the promise, and feed on it.

We see then, that the devil takes the word from their hearts. The word is a seed that must be planted in the heart. We're not talking about the physical heart that pumps blood. We're talking about the spirit of man. The words 'spirit' and 'heart' are interchangeable. The seed cannot be planted in the physical heart of man. Neither can the word of God be planted into the big toe of a man. It's got to go into the spirit of the man. That's what the Bible refers to, the spirit of the man, or the heart of the man.

> **Mark 4:15 (NKJ)** *And these are the ones by the* **wayside** *where the word is sown. When they hear, Satan comes* **immediately** *and takes away the word that was sown* **in** *their hearts.*

Now, family, why is the devil so keen to take the word, out of the heart of a person who receives it, immediately? Why does he come immediately to take the word? It seems like the devil is anxious to get the word, if he desires to come immediately. In fact I would say that he's paranoid. I dare say that the devil knows something about the value and power and ability of that word that Christians don't. No one knows more about the word of God than God. The devil is second in terms of knowledge, and third is the church, which is beginning to find something out. Why is the devil so paranoid about the word, family? Without the word we are powerless.

> **James 1:6 (NKJ)** *But let him ask in faith, with no doubting...*
>
> *[7] For let not that man suppose that he will receive anything from the Lord (without faith);*

35

> Without faith I cannot receive anything from the
> Lord.

I've seen people die who love God with all their hearts, and they die saying, *"I love you Jesus, I love you Jesus."* I know God was desperate to raise them up, but without faith it is impossible to receive anything from the Lord and Satan knows that. Satan brings problems to us and these problems, whatever they might be, sickness, financial challenges, family challenges, spiritual challenges, are intended to hold us in bondage and steal the word. Satan wants to be lord over the church. He wants to control the church. He wants to control our lives. He wants to control everything. But he can't. We can hold him captive with our words. We get rid of his problems with the word of God. We stay in charge and the devil stays under our feet.

Jesus said, *"You will walk on serpents and tread on scorpions and over all the power of the enemy"* (**Luke 10:9**), but we can't do that if we don't have the word in us. We don't walk on the devil with our feet. We walk on the devil with our words, which come out of the abundance of the heart. Satan knows if he can steal the word, he can steal God's help from us. If he can steal the word he can hold us captive. If he can steal the word he can keep us helpless. We will be limited only to our natural resources if he can steal the word. Family, the word is extremely important and we have to understand that. These truths are all important, but there are two truths in this portion of scripture that are the most valuable. We dare not miss these two truths if we expect to understand all of the other parables.

Number one — God's word is valuable. The **second** truth is we must understand the law of sowing and reaping. Every word I say is a seed planted and the harvest comes. That's a law we must understand.

> The word of God is vital to my success. Every word
> I say is a seed planted and the harvest comes.

The whole of God's kingdom works by seed time and harvest. Everything God created came from seed (spoken words). All animals reproduce by seeds, all the plant life reproduces by seeds. There will be time between the sowing of the seed and the harvesting of the crop. Time will pass. The Bible said, there will be 'seed time and harvest.' But we must keep watering the seed with our praise, and act like it's true. We cannot say it's true and then act like it's not true.

> ***Mark 4:16 (NKJ)*** *These likewise are the ones sown on **stony ground** who, when they hear the word, immediately receive it with gladness;*
>
> *[17] and they have no root in themselves, and so endure only for a time. Afterward, when **tribulation***

> *or **persecution arises for the word's sake**,*
> *immediately they stumble.*

Here we see Satan brings tribulation and persecution for the word's sake. The devil doesn't bring problems our way just because he doesn't like us. Sure he doesn't like us, but the main reason he brings problems our way, such as tribulations, persecutions, people saying things about us, is for the word's sake. Satan wants to steal the word, and to prevent us from getting into the word. As a result, we have many problems in our life and we find that we can't read our Bible. We can't listen to teachings. We can't go to church because we've got tribulations.

"Oh, but Pastor Theo I don't have time to read the word because I've got so many things going on I have to fix." We can't see beyond the natural because the devil is causing the problems to keep us out of the word. The way to solve that is not by trying to solve the problems, but by getting into the word and going the way of the word to solve the problems. Put the word into yourself and speak to those problems. You can't dig and shovel the mountain away. You have to speak to it. Jesus didn't say, *"if you go out there and attack the mountain, and move it with a grader it will move."* He said, *"talk to it."*

David said, *"Goliath, this day the Lord will give you into my hand."* He used his words and God took the sling and destroyed Goliath.

We have to speak to our mountain and our problems and use our words, which come out of a heart that is filled with the word. Then God will use who and what He needs to, if He chooses to do it that way.

We all know people who don't have the time because they have too many problems. They try to take short-cuts instead of the right way, which is the word. Can you imagine if someone said to me, *"I don't have time to walk down the steps, so I will just jump off the platform."* They jump and break their leg! Now they've got all the time in the world to lie in the hospital with a broken leg. Suddenly, they found some time. **We may not have time to read the word, but we have time to tend the problems that the word would have solved**.

> We may not have time to read the word, but we have time to tend the problems that the word would have solved.

This particular ground, **the stony ground**, is a little better than the **wayside** soil. Then we move on to the **thorny soil**, which is a small improvement on the stony ground. We're getting closer to what we should be.

> ***Mark 4:18 (NKJ)*** *Now these are the ones sown among thorns; they are the ones who hear the word,*

Notice each time they hear the word,

> *¹⁹ and the cares of this world, the **deceitfulness of riches**, and the **desires for other things** entering in choke the word, and it becomes unfruitful.*

The Bible talks about the deceitfulness of riches. What does that mean? That means we have to understand the place of money in our lives.

Say this, 'God is number one. Financial blessings are **not** number one in my life.'

The word has to be number one. Financial prosperity is a blessing of the Lord. We are not to seek money in such a way that we don't have time for God. The deceitfulness of riches puts its value of money in the wrong place. There are certain things money cannot do for us. **Money is a great blessing from the Lord, but money is a lousy god.** People who have their priorities mixed up, say things like, *"We cannot come to church on Sundays, Pastor Theo, because we've got this expensive boat, and it's a waste of money if we don't use it. So we go water-skiing every Sunday. I'll try and get to church this year. All right Pastor Theo, love you. Remember me in your prayers while I'm skiing on Sunday."* I would like to say, "Sure. I will remember you in my prayers, 'Lord, break his leg!'" Only kidding!

Say this, *"I must not allow the pleasures of the world, that the Lord buys for me, to steal my time from reading the Bible, listening to good teachings, and going to church."*

The Bible says in the last days people will be lovers of pleasure more than lovers of God. Let's not allow that to happen to us. We can see the devil is the one behind this. We have to be careful that our possessions do not steal our time from God's word.

> **Mark 4:20 (NKJ)** *But these are the ones sown on* **good ground**, *those who* **hear** *the word,* **accept** *it, and bear fruit: some thirtyfold, some sixty, and some a hundred.*

How do they bear the good fruit? They **hear** the word and they **do** it.

Say this, *"The Lord Jesus said, 'I must be careful* **how I hear***, and how I listen.' Take heed how you hear."*

All of us plant a garden. All of us are farmers, and we need to prepare the soil of our heart to receive God's seed — God's word. The seed is incorruptible, and it can never fail. The reason the seed doesn't produce its harvest is because of the soil's condition. All of the seeds are the same, but the condition of the soil makes a difference.

> **Wayside** soil, same seed, it can't produce.
> **Stony** soil, same seed, it can't produce.
> **Thorny** soil, same seed, it can't produce.

Some soils produce 30, 60, and 100-fold. It is the same seed, but it produces a different harvest. If there's a problem with our faith, it is not the seed, it is the heart. We are to make sure our heart is ready for the seed, all the time. Turn over the soil, and pull out the weeds. Develop a hunger for God's word. What are the weeds then? Bitterness, resentment, **jealousy**, unforgiveness, pride, etc. These things are deadly weeds in our garden that choke the word and prevent God's word from producing its harvest in our lives. When we allow all that in, we are sacrificing the abundant blessings of God. It's not worth it. We cannot afford financially to allow unforgiveness, bitterness, resentment, and jealousy in our heart. We can't afford it physically. The price is too much to pay with our physical health to entertain those things. They cut off the blessings of God; the devil uses those things to choke out the word.

If there's a problem with my faith, it's the soil, not God's seed.

We need to listen, listen, listen, listen. Give attention to the word. If we listen to everything else around us, watching TV all day, watching every new movie that comes out, soaking it all in, I can tell you right now, eventually we will become hypnotized to accepting all the garbage that goes into our heart. It will produce a bad harvest in our lives.

Some years ago the mother of one of our pastors, a dear old saint, was about 90 years old and was dying. She was in and out of a comatose state. In the hospital she cursed incessantly, using all sorts of four letter words that would make a sailor blush. I wouldn't dare want to remember them. But here was this beautiful saint of God, cursing and swearing. This couple came to me and said they were shocked and embarrassed because all the hospital staff knew that they were pastors and that their mom was also a Christian, and yet she was using such bad language.

I asked , *"Did your mother spend a lot of time watching movies."*

"Oh, she loved movies, watched movies all day," they said.

Guess what was in her heart? Now it was coming out of her mouth.

Whatever we give our ears to goes into our hearts. Our hearts are soil. It will plant anything we put in it. Just hit your thumbnail by accident, and see what comes out of your mouth. You'll find out what's in your heart. That gets in there by what we listen to. Take heed how you hear, Jesus said.

> Whatever I give my ear to goes into my heart. My heart is soil. It will plant anything I put in it.

1 Peter 1:23 tells us God's word is incorruptible seed. Let's go to **Matthew 12:35**, where Jesus is speaking.

> ***Matthew 12:35 (NKJ)*** *A good man out of the good treasure of his heart brings forth good things, and an evil man out of the evil treasure brings forth evil things.*

What is that good treasure in the good man's heart? The word of God.

Say this, *"I must treasure God's word. It must be more important than my nice cars, my nice home, and all my blessings."* The word of God must be a greater treasure than anything else before it will produce its harvest.

We must treasure God's word.

If I don't value the word, then I won't read it or meditate in it, then it's not treasure to me. If everything else is more important, and I say, 'Oh I didn't have time to get into the word today, but I'll try and find a little time tomorrow,' it's not a treasure. We can't expect any kind of great harvest to come up. That's fine if that happens once in a while, but if that is a normal situation that is a problem.

I cannot emphasize how important this is — **the word of God is a seed in the heart that produces a good harvest in our lives**. That's why God said the good man out of the good treasure of his heart brings forth good things.

Question, who brings forth the good things, God or the man? The man. That's what God said.

We can therefore believe and say with confidence, "Every need that I will ever have, financially, spiritually, mentally, physically, health-wise, family-wise, everything I need, God has already given to me. It is in my hand in seed form. He has given me all the seeds I need for every harvest. I am a farmer and I must never complain about the prosperous farm next to me, if I have all my seeds in the barn instead of in the field."

Stop whining, and plant the seed. Don't go stand at the neighbor's fence and say, *"Wah wah wah wahah."* Just get out there and plant your own seed. A good man out of the good treasure of his heart brings forth good things. An evil man out of the evil treasure brings forth evil things. Did God bring the evil things on the man? Did the devil? Did the man? The Bible says the evil man out of the evil treasure of his heart brings forth the evil things. The devil brings evil things, but so does the man. He compounds the problem. The devil does something bad and the man says, *"Well I'm having a bad day. It looks like it's going to get worse tomorrow. And I'm so worried, even God's worried."* The man opens the door for the devil and says, *"Come right in Mr. Devil, do your thing."*

> **Proverbs 4:23 (NIV)** *Above all else, guard your heart, for it is the wellspring of life.*

If God says we've got to look after something that means it is important. He's given us many things to look after. But the one we have to protect more than anything else is our heart. Now what would **we** think is the most important thing we have to protect? *"Pastor Theo, somebody said I have to take care of my assets. I have to watch the stock market day and night."* Another said, *"I have to watch over my family."* No, we are missing the mark. God said we are to guard the heart because it is the wellspring of life. In other words, all our success, all our health, all our prosperity, and all our happiness comes out of the heart. If we neglect our heart, we are neglecting our assets. If we neglect our heart, we are neglecting our family. If we neglect our heart, we are neglecting our business. If we neglect our heart, we are neglecting our own happiness because all of these come out of our heart. The soil is the place that produces all of that.

> If I neglect my heart, I neglect my own happiness because everything I need comes out of my heart.

A few years ago when I was on a trip to South Africa, I went to Cape Town to minister for Pastor Allan Bagg for a day or two. He asked, *"Where would you like to go to lunch Pastor Theo?"* I remembered this beautiful restaurant that makes Lobster Thermidor. They take a 4-pound lobster, remove all the meat and then cook it in a brandy sauce. They put cheese on it and then brown it in the oven, burning all the alcohol out at the same time. Then they put the meat back inside the lobster shell and they bring the two halves, beautifully displayed on a plate, and you think you have died and gone to heaven.

I said, *"I want to go to that restaurant."* We got there and I looked at the menu, and saw my choice was on the menu, so I closed it. James, the waiter, came to the table and said, *"Right, these are the specials."*

I said, *"Don't tell me about any specials just get me the Lobster Thermidor."*

He said, *"I'm sorry to tell you sir, it's not the season for lobster. There are no lobsters anywhere. You can't fish for lobsters right now. It's not allowed and there are just no lobsters anywhere. What else would you like?"*

I said, *"Look, I'll tell you what. There's a brand new lobster that has just arrived. It's in the kitchen right now."* He just looked at me. So I said to him, *"I have inside information, The Lord Jesus knew I was coming here to get this lobster today and it's waiting for me."* He looked at me as if to say, 'what planet do you come from?'

I said, *"Do me a favor, go and look."* Off he went and returned with a shocked look on his face.

He said, *"There is one magnificent lobster in the kitchen. I don't know how it got there."*

I said, *"Well it's mine. Jesus has it there for me."* And they gave it to me.

Remember, you have what you say.

Jesus is ready to confirm the word of God spoken with signs following.

- I am blessed coming in and blessed going out.
- I am blessed in the city.
- I am blessed in the field.
- I'm above only, not beneath.
- I'm a winner.
- I am highly favored.
- I'm blessed and highly favored. Everybody wants to do things for me wherever I go. They love me, want to help me, and want to bless me. They want to give things to me.
- Everywhere I go I get discounts. I am blessed to be a blessing to others. I am blessed to be a greater influence for the gospel of Jesus.

Chapter Three

The Condition Of Our Heart

> *Matthew 12:35 (NKJ) A **good man**, out of the good treasure of his heart brings forth good things, and an evil man out of the evil treasure (of his heart) brings forth evil things.*

Where do the good things come from? The heart. The heart is like soil. The heart produces the harvest. Does the verse say that **God** brought forth the good things or is it the **man** who brought forth the good things?

You must say, "**It's up to me to go farming with the seed I have been given.**"

The soil brings forth the harvest, it doesn't matter what happens in life, we can never blame the seed for not producing the harvest. It's the heart that's at fault if the harvest doesn't come. Jesus gave the example in **Mark 4** about the different soils; **wayside** soil, **stony** soil, **thorny** soil, the three different categories of **good** soil, which produce 30, 60 and 100 fold returns. The exact same seed was planted in all those soils, but produced different results. God's seed is divine and will always produce if the soil allows.

'Light be', produced the sun and all the stars and all that we see out in space. That creative power is captive in every seed. But it can't produce its harvest unless it goes into our heart. We need to take care of our heart, look after it, prepare its soil, pull out the weeds, and make sure it is fertile land so we can receive a harvest.

> **Proverbs 4:23 (NIV)** *Above all else, guard your heart, for it is the wellspring of life.*

We all have assets to take care of, whether they are financial, family or the possessions we have bought. If we want to take care of those assets properly, we need to take care of our heart. All those blessings we have in the natural realm came to us through the heart. The Bible tells us that the heart is the wellspring of life. What does wellspring mean? The desert is dry, barren, and nothing grows. In **Genesis 26** we learnt that Isaac dug out the wells that his father Abraham first dug many years before. Those wells started producing fresh water. If you went out into the desert and found a well, you'd probably find palm trees, you'd find fruit trees, vegetable gardens, and a little village of people gathered with their camels. There's life going on, a little town, all because of the well. The water brought forth that life that we see in that little oasis.

Your heart is the well and out of your heart springs forth all the things we have in the natural. If you stop the water flowing out of the well, soon enough the palm trees die, the fruit trees die, the vegetables die and the camels and the people leave and you'd have desert again. So, if we forgot about taking care of that well in the desert, and only looked after the camels, the vegetables and the palm trees, and ignored the well so that it slowly died, and stopped producing water, we would be stupid.

When we neglect our Bible reading, when we neglect going to church, when we neglect listening to teachings, and hearing the word of God, we are ignoring the well. That's very serious. That's ignorance gone to seed.

Jesus said, 'take heed **how** you hear' (**Luke 8:18**). You don't want to hear just anything. There are many things we don't want to listen to, on TV and movies, discussions in the office, and life in general. There's a lot of stuff that we don't want to listen to, because it's going to get into our soil and mess up our production center.

If you owned that oasis out in the middle of the desert, you wouldn't let some traveller take poison and throw it down your well. You'd go after him and teach him a lesson he would never forget because he has just killed everything in your whole village. Why would you let somebody poison your well?

> "My heart is the most important treasure that I have.
> It's my production center. It's my factory producing God's blessings."

Matthew 12:35 (NKJ) *A good man, out of the good treasure of his heart brings forth good things.*

I wonder if this is true? I wonder if God knows what He is talking about? **Did God** bring the evil into this man's life? Did **the devil** bring the evil into this man's life? **The man** did. Certainly the devil can bring evil into anybody's life if we'll let him. But we don't need to **help** him! The **evil man** brought forth the evil. The **good man** brings forth the good out of the good treasure in his heart. What is the treasure that brings forth this good?

Say this, 'the word of God is a treasure. The seed is the treasure. If I don't treasure God's word, I'll never plant it. I must understand God's word is treasure.'

We're all looking for treasure, and we walk right past it. The word is the treasure, and it produces its harvest. God has given us a key. If you don't understand this parable you won't understand any other parables.

> The word of God is a treasure. The seed is the treasure. If I don't treasure God's word, I'll never plant it. I must understand God's word is treasure.

The evil man produces the evil things. How?

> **Matthew 12:36 (NKJ)** *But I say to you that for every idle word men may speak, they will give account of it in the day of judgment.*

The evil treasure of the evil man's heart comes forth because he speaks idle words. What's an idle word? If somebody refused to go out and find a job, and insisted on staying home, watching TV all day, and all night, we would say that that person is idle, or lazy. He needs to get off his blessed assurance and go and look for a job. So, an idle word then, is a word that's not productive. It's not extending God's kingdom; it's not furthering God's cause and it's not being a blessing. A productive word is a word that brings bless-ing. A non-productive word is a word that does nothing. There's no purpose. Now we do have to carry on everyday business and normal conversation. But a non-productive word is a word that contradicts the word of God, or goes against the word of God. A word of doubt, unbelief, fear, or something the word of God disapproves of is a non-productive idle word. If we talk like that, we are going to produce problems in our life. That's why we have to look after our words, and be careful how we speak. We are inclined to set our standards by what we see around us in the world and not set our standards by the word of God. We'd rather go by, 'everybody's doing it so it's okay.' That's the thing we told our parents and that's the thing our kids tell us. 'Everybody's doing this, it's okay.' It's not okay with God.

Say this, *"I will set my standards by what the word says, and not by what the world says."*

The world's value of words and God's value of words are different as night is from day. God values His word even more than He values His own name. Is your name important to you? Absolutely! Is your word more important to you than your name? If it's not, we've got the cart before the horse. God's word is more important to Him than His name. You see, God's name is important because His words are important.

Say this, *"I am only as good as my word. My name is only worth the integrity of my word. If my word is no good, my name is no good."*

The Bible said there are one or two things God can't do. One is He can't lie. What does that mean? That means when God says it, He will do it, He will abide by it. I can tell you right now, God will keep His word even if nobody else does. He will never break His word. People have said, *"God is sovereign He can do what He wants."* Yes, but in eternity past God knew what He was going to say, and He made a decision to be sovereign about that statement and abide by it for eternity. So before He said it, He thought about it, and He made the statement, which He is going to live by and not break for eternity. God refuses to break His Word because He and His word are one. Now the devil will break his word on every turn. And where do we stand? We are somewhere in between. We should try and value God's word the way He does, and our words too, because He is our example. We can't speak haphazardly and foolishly, and thoughtlessly, and think we're going to be a mighty man or woman of faith. We are not.

Say this, "**Words are divine instruments of creation that God has entrusted to me**."

I must be careful how I use them. You see, we are created in the image and likeness of God. God is a spirit being and you are a spirit being created in the image and likeness of God (**Genesis 1:26**). You live in a physical body. God is a creator and you are a creator. Only mankind was given the power to create. God says you can have what you say (**Mark 11:23**).

> Words are divine instruments of creation that God
> has entrusted to me.

Say this, *"I am supposed to frame my world with my words like God framed the universe with His words."* And what must our world look like? It must look like what God says.

Say this, *"I am to speak healing when sickness comes. I am to speak prosperity when poverty comes. I am to speak love when strife comes. I am to speak blessing when lack comes. I am to speak, 'I hear God's voice,' when confusion comes. I am to speak all the good things of God to bring in God's plans, God's purposes, in a world that Satan is trying to destroy.* **I must allow God to reign through my words in my world.**"

Hearts that are ready to hear God's word, and speak God's word, will produce God's blessings in their circle of influence. That's why America is so prosperous. There were hearts that God could work through. God cannot bless any nation, or anyone, unless He blesses through the heart of the man or woman by words spoken. That's why in countries where Jesus is not Lord, and the word of God is not present, that country suffers crime, strife, and poverty because there are no hearts where the word can be planted.

> Hearts that are ready to hear God's word, and speak God's word, will produce God's blessings in their circle of influence.

We must not close up our well. We must allow God to work through us by speaking His word. We have a divine instrument of creative power given to us, God's word. Let us look on the other side of the coin for a moment — at the power of negative confession. Let's see what happens when people say things they shouldn't say. We don't want to dwell in the negative camp, but just look at it so we can more effectively apply positive confession in the positive camp.

> ***Ephesians 5:1 (NIV)*** *Be imitators of God, therefore, as dearly loved children*
>
> *[2] and live a life of love, just as Christ loved us and gave himself up for us as a fragrant offering and sacrifice to God.*
>
> *[3] But among you…*

Among who? The children of God. *"Among you, children of God* **there must not be…***."* He didn't say if you feel like it. He said there must not be even a hint. Don't even talk about it.

> *[3] But among you there must not be even a hint of sexual immorality, or of any kind of impurity, or of greed, because these are improper for God's holy people.*
>
> *[4] Nor should there be obscenity,* **foolish talk***, or coarse joking, which are out of place, but rather thanksgiving."*

In the same group as all these terrible sins and sinful ways, is this statement, '**foolish talk**'. The world does not understand that foolish talk is as bad as these other things but God sees it **as bad**. Foolish talk is extremely dangerous and can cause a lot of damage. Just like a cigarette can burn acres of forests, so our tongue can destroy lives, send people to hell, cause sickness, and produce poverty in a flourishing business. It can destroy churches; it can destroy families, and cause divorce. It can cause death at an early age. Our tongue has extreme negative abilities. Therefore, foolish talk is something we want to stay away from even more than the other things that are listed in the scripture. Let the world think, 'I can say what I want to, any time I want to, I always speak my mind, rhubarb, rhubarb, rhubarb,' and off they go. You've heard the saying, 'empty cans make the most noise.' The world doesn't mind speaking foolishly, but God warns us not to. Will you consider the consequences of this?

I have been in the company of people who spoke thoughtlessly, Christians who criticize other Christians. I can assure you, I've sensed the Holy Spirit grieving at that moment and extreme pain entered my heart. People who speak foolishly and jokingly and criticize, and say things they shouldn't say, seem to be oblivious of the consequences of what they are doing to themselves, and the hurt that they're bringing on themselves. We are to speak the word of God and we are to speak in line with the word of God.

What the world considers to be acceptable conversation is often not acceptable to God, and we are not to lower our standards to those around us. If we're going to walk in faith we are going to have to step it up a few notches when it comes to watching our words. Through the years I've learnt that the less I speak, the less I sin. The less I speak, the fewer mistakes I make, and the less I have to repent of. We should think before we speak, because we are planting seeds, and all those words go into our heart.

> **James 1:26 (NKJ)** *If anyone among you thinks he is religious, and does not bridle his tongue but* **deceives his own heart,** *this one's religion is useless.*

James is writing to Christians under the inspiration of the Holy Ghost. He says, 'if there is any Christian among you who thinks he's religious or thinks he's a good Christian but **doesn't bridle his tongue, he deceives his own heart**.' In other words, a person is not a good Christian if he doesn't control his tongue. **A tongue that speaks carelessly will deceive the heart into error**. I know many Christians who are deceived, they have deceived themselves to believe error, to believe incorrectly. We have to speak in line with the word. If we say things that are out of order with the word we will start believing it. Our heart is like soil,it will grow whatever we plant in it. If you plant carrots and you plant weeds at the same time, both will grow. You would not know which is which for a time. You might pull up carrots by mistake. In the same way, if we plant junk in our hearts, family, we're going to confuse our whole life. We can never walk in great faith when we're confused.

> **Romans 12:1 (NKJ)** *I beseech you therefore, brethren, by the mercies of God, that you present your bodies a living sacrifice, holy, acceptable to God, which is your reasonable service.*
>
> *² And do not be conformed to this world, but be transformed by the renewing of your mind, that you may prove what is that good and acceptable and perfect will of God.*

Our thinking is renewed (corrected) by reading the word. Why? That you may prove what is the good and acceptable and perfect will of God. There are three different categories or degrees of God's will, and if I know the word and understand the truth of God's word, then I'm able to speak in line with God's word. I can allow truth to enter my heart, which will empower me to walk in God's will.

Say this, *"I believe I hear God's voice, I walk in His will. I receive direction and I obey that direction. I declare God orders my steps."* When we say something like that, we are allowing God to direct our lives.

I believe I hear God's voice, and I walk in His will. I receive direction and I obey that direction. I declare God orders my steps.

Error would be if you said something like this, *"I don't know what I'm going to do now. This is so confusing. I don't know what to do."* Or, *"I don't know where that thing is. It's lost, it's probably gone forever."* Or, *"It's a hopeless mess. We'll never solve this problem."* Because we don't know God heals we say that God doesn't heal. We bring error to our heart and we walk out of the will of God in that area. A tongue that's not bridled will deceive the heart.

Say this, *"my born again heart can believe a lie."* And, *"my words determine what I believe."*

If we hold fast to our confession of faith, *"By Jesus' stripes I am healed, by Jesus' stripes I am healed, by Jesus' stripes I am healed,"* and then we say, *"I'm waiting for this pain to go away,"* we have just confused our spirit. Our actions need to line up with our confession of faith. Our actions confirm what we believe.

A bridle is used to control a horse, in the same way we need to bridle our tongue.

> **James 3:1 (NKJ)** *My brethren, let not many of you become teachers, knowing that we shall receive a stricter judgment.*
>
> ² *For we all stumble in many things.* **If anyone does not stumble in word**, *he is a perfect man,* **able also to bridle the whole body.**

Don't let that word **perfect** throw you. The Greek says, '**to be full grown in spiritual maturity**.' Therefore, let us read it this way: *"...anyone who does not stumble in his words is a full grown mature Christian."* That means someone who doesn't speak irresponsibly, carelessly or thoughtlessly, but has control over his words. Someone who speaks carelessly and is always fooling around and does not think before they speak is a baby Christian, not full grown in spiritual maturity.

"If anyone does not stumble in word he is a perfect man." That means if we don't say things that contradict the Bible, if we speak in line with the word, or say things that harmonize with the word, we are a perfect man. The Bible says a man like that can bridle the whole body. What does that mean? That means that our words control our physical body. If there's something wrong with our body, and we bridle our words and say, *"by Jesus' stripes I am healed,"* the body will bridle up to being healed.

If there's anything in our life that we aren't pleased with — any habit we have that we want to get rid of — if there's anything in our house, our bedroom, our life, our office we are responsible for, that we are not pleased with — let's check our words to find out why it is like that, because the Bible says our words bridle our body. Our words, therefore, bridle our house, our home, our children, our family, and our life. Just like a bit in a horse's mouth directs where the horse goes, our words direct where we go.

Say this, *"my tongue directs my life, and sets my course."*

> [3] *Indeed we put bits in horses' mouths that they may obey us and we turn their whole body.*

We have to start training a horse when it is a foal. When it is tiny, put the bit in its mouth and train it. It takes time before that horse listens. We have to take time to consciously train ourselves to speak words of faith, to speak positively, to speak the word of God, to stay in line with the word. It's not by accident. If we wait until the horse is 15 years old, it's not going to start listening to us the moment we bridle it. The Bible says we put bits in horses' mouths that they may obey us, and then we can turn their whole body. The whole horse will listen and it will go wherever we want it to go.

> **James 3:4 (NKJ)** *Look also at ships: although they are so large and are driven by fierce winds, they are turned by a very small rudder wherever the pilot desires.*

Some cruise ships out on the ocean can carry thousands of people and resemble giant hotels. When you compare the size of that ship to the small rudder that steers it, it's amazing. No matter how bad the storm is, the captain just turns that wheel and the ship will turn. But it doesn't turn straight away. He turns that wheel and slowly but surely thousands of tons of water begin to move and that ship starts to turn, little by little. No matter how bad the storm is, the captain can get the ship safely into harbor.

Say this, *"It doesn't matter how bad the storms of life are if I will hold fast to my confession of faith my tongue will take me, with God's guidance through the storms of life and I will always arrive in the harbor of God's blessing. God has a way. He is a way maker and he's taking me through."*

> **James 3:3 (NKJ)** *Indeed we put bits in horses' mouths that they may obey us and we turn their whole body.*
>
> *[4] Look also at ships: although they are so large and are driven by fierce winds, they are turned by a very small rudder wherever the pilot desires.*
>
> *[5] Even so the tongue...*

James is saying that just like the bit turns the horse, and just like the rudder turns the ship, so the tongue will turn our life around. If there's any part of our life that we're not happy with, the tongue is where we need to look for our solution.

It doesn't matter how bad the storms of life are, if I will hold fast to my confession of faith my tongue will take me, with God's guidance through the storms of life and I will always arrive in the harbor of God's blessing.

Say this, *"I am blessed coming in. I am blessed going out. I am highly favored of God. I have favor with men. Everybody wants to help me. Everybody wants to bless me."*

*"By Jesus' stripes I **was** healed and I **am** healed and I walk in perfect health all my life. Jesus keeps me well and He is the strength of my life."*

"I declare I hear God's voice and I obey His voice. He is ordering my steps and I am walking in the perfect will of God every day. I am fulfilling His plan for my life. I am completing my destiny and my assignment for this life. God is keeping me holy and faithful. He is keeping me in His perfect will, in Jesus' name."

"In Jesus' name, my children are blessed. There is harmony and love in my home. Strife does not exist in my house. We are all living under the influence of God. Satan has no influence in our house. Angels live in our home day and night. We are protected. Everything we do, everywhere we go, we are protected. Angels go with us. They go before us."

"God is going ahead of me. He's organizing my future. The people I meet, things I do, He has prepared my way. When I get there it's all arranged. Things are happening. They are waiting just for me to arrive. In the name of Jesus everything is going my way because everything is going God's way and I'm walking in His way."

Family, it does not take long to program our heart, or to program our spirit and plant good seed. Let's not root it up and say things that contradict those words. When we meet somebody say, *"Praise God I am blessed and highly favored. By Jesus' stripes I am healed and I walk in divine health. I hear God's voice and I walk in His perfect plan. How are you?"*

Chapter Four

What God's Kingdom Looks Like

Although it is impossible to live a successful Christian life without understanding the power of positive words, we do need to realize that there is more to our walk with the Lord than just positive words. Other things are also necessary. For example, if you look at a chain, you will see it has many links. The power of positive words would be one of those links. Hearing God's voice is another link. We could be believing God to go north and God wants us to go south. We need to be sure that we know what God wants for our lives and then confess that. If we focus on only one aspect of our walk we become lopsided Christians. The Bible is clear on many different subjects, such as healing. We don't have to ask whether it's God's will to heal us because the Bible tells us it is. We don't have to ask whether it's God's will for us to prosper financially because the Bible tells us it is.

The word of God is not clear when it comes to personal issues. For example, *"Joe Soap, you should go and preach in China."* You need to hear God's voice and then confess, *"Praise God. It's God's will and I'm going to preach in China, He's going to make a way."* But don't confess that if it's **not** God's will, or you don't know.

Let's look at what the kingdom of God is. Bear in mind at the beginning of **Mark 4**, Jesus said, *"If you do not understand this parable you will not understand any other parables in the Bible."* This is the foundation upon which everything else is based. So it's imperative that we understand **Mark 4**. If I asked you to paint a picture in your mind of what the kingdom of heaven looks like, what would your picture be? Or, if I asked you to paint a picture of the kingdom of God in action, what kind of picture would you have in your mind? Let's ask the Lord Jesus, because He answers that question right here in:

> **Mark 4:26 (NKJ)** *And He said, "The kingdom of God is as if a man should scatter seed on the ground."*

Can you see a man with a bag of corn seed, on his farm out in the field, scattering seed as He walks? Jesus is telling us that this is a picture of the kingdom of God. If you want to understand what the kingdom of God looks like, that's the picture. With our natural thinking mind we cannot wrap our brain around that. We have to put ourselves in God's shoes to understand what He's saying. God is saying that everything in His kingdom works through seed time and harvest. Everything is a seed. Not only the corn we sow, not only people producing people through seed, and animals producing animals through seed, and fruit trees producing fruit trees through seed; but everything you sow is a seed and every action you do is a seed. The love you give is a seed that comes back to you.

Now say this, *"Every seed produces after its kind. That means love brings back love."*

It's no wonder that when God wanted an eternal family in heaven, He made the decision to plant a seed to receive an eternal family. He decided to give His only son in order to reap a harvest of many sons and many daughters.

How does a seed function? It first has to die and then be put in the ground. That's what happened to Jesus. He died and then He was buried. Then it brings forth its harvest. Likewise, all of us have come forth out of Jesus, that seed. None of us would be here today if it weren't for the death, burial and resurrection of our Lord Jesus, our Savior. He entered our hearts with His life. Therefore you could quite easily say that it is true that we are all of the Lord Jesus, the original seed.

The Lord Jesus Himself says this in:

> **John 12:23 (NLT)** *Jesus replied that the time had come for Him to return to His glory in heaven*
>
> [24] *and that I must fall and die like a kernel of wheat that falls into the furrows of the earth lest I die I will be alone, a single seed. But my death will produce many new wheat kernels, a plentiful harvest of new lives.*

All translations use the word 'seed' in **John 12:24**. Therefore, God planted His only son as a seed to reap a harvest of many children, and we have all come forth out of that orig-

69

inal seed. Family, that is huge! God decided to bring forth an eternal family through sowing and reaping. I'm sure in His infinite knowledge, He could have chosen another way to accomplish that. But He chose sowing and reaping, and that's important for us to understand. Jesus said the kingdom of God is sowing and reaping. Even populating heaven has come as a result of sowing and reaping.

> **Matthew 7:12 (NKJ)** *Therefore whatever you want men to do to you, do also to them, for this is the law and the prophets.*

The Lord Jesus says that whatever we want men to do to us, do to them, for this is the law and the prophets. What does this mean, '**this is the law and the prophets**'? The law refers to Moses' first five books of the Old Testament, the law. The prophets refer to the other books of the Old Testament written after the law by the other prophets. This takes care of the entire Old Testament. Jesus explains that the entire Old Testament is captured in this one verse. The Old Testament message is, '**do unto others what you want them to do to you**.'

What does this all mean? It means **sowing and reaping**. That is the law of seed time and harvest. That is the law of sowing seeds. That is the kingdom of heaven principle, a man sowing seed. Bear in mind, this is mentioned in **Matthew 7**, right at the beginning of the New Testament. So, right from the beginning, Jesus makes it clear that the principle He is teaching is, 'do unto others as you want them to do to you.' This is the message of this new covenant that Jesus is teaching. But He also says, 'this is the message of the Old Testament.'

> The Old Testament is actually the New Testament hidden away.
> The New Testament is actually the Old Testament revealed.

We see the picture gets even bigger. Sowing and reaping is more involved and far extended from what we first imagined. Not only is it populating heaven, but it is our life on the earth. **All creation**, **all progress**, **all growth is through seed**. **First**, is God's creation. **Second**, the earth is populated through seed. **Third**, **we** create **our** world, and we bring into order God's plans into our world by planting seed. **By speaking words we are planting seeds**. The Bible tells us that God's word is incorruptible seed (**1 Peter 1:23**). It says the same thing in **Luke 8** and in **Mark 4**.

Everything we say is a seed that goes into the heart of man, which is soil. It goes into the heart and germinates and produces a harvest. Whatever we say will come back to us in the form of a harvest. So then, we must create our world with our words, the same way that God created His world with His words. For our words are seeds and His words are seeds. We plant them the way God planted His. God created everything through words.

> **Genesis 1:3 (NKJ)** *Then God said, "Let there be light"; and there was light.*

God spoke the sun into existence. The sun came out of a seed, and that seed was the word '**light be**', spoken from God's mouth.

> *⁹ Then God said, "Let the waters of the heavens be gathered together into one place and let the dry land appear"; and it was so.*

The water and the dry land appeared because of the spoken **word**, the **seed** that was planted.

> *¹¹ Then God said, "Let the earth bring forth grass, the herb that yields seed, and the fruit tree that yields fruit according to its kind, whose seed is in itself, on the earth"; and it was so.*

God said it and there it was. Therefore everything in existence began with **words**. Everything in existence began with **seeds**. In **Mark 16** the Lord Jesus told us to go and preach the gospel to every creature.

> **Mark 16:20 (NKJ)** *And they went out and preached everywhere, the Lord working with them and confirming the word through the accompanying signs.*

The disciples went out and preached the gospel everywhere, and Jesus worked with them; everything they preached, Jesus acted on and manifested. When they preached healing, healing came. When they preached salvation, salvation came. When they preached being full of the Holy Ghost, people began to speak in tongues.

That's why, in churches where the gospel of Salvation is not preached, people might not even believe in Jesus as their Savior. They might preach politics, the latest secular book review, but nothing from the Bible. The folks in that church will not even have salvation because the message of salvation is not being preached. This seed for salvation must go out before you can see the harvest of salvation.

Then you can go to some churches where they believe in salvation, but they don't believe that folks can be filled with the Holy Spirit, because some churches don't believe healing is for today. They don't teach it, no word goes out so healing doesn't manifest. Many are sick in that church. Healing doesn't manifest. Then you go to some churches that never preach Biblical prosperity. Many in that church live in poverty. They might even take a vow of poverty.

Unless the word goes out first, there's nothing for God to confirm, because the seed must be planted before the harvest comes forth. That's why Jesus said. *"Go out and preach the gospel."* Through sowing the seed of salvation into the hearts of humanity, there was a harvest of salvations, and the church was born. The body of Christ was born.

Today **we** must shape **our** world with **our** words the way God shaped this universe with His words. We must speak forth the blessings of God that were paid for at Calvary. When sickness comes we have to declare, *"By Jesus' stripes I was healed."* When poverty comes in the front door, we have to open the door and say, *"God meets all my needs according to His riches in glory by Christ Jesus."* When strife comes knocking on the front door, we have to go to the front door and say, *"Peace, harmony and love abide in this home."* We have to speak God's purposes and plans into our lives. If we don't, it won't happen.

If it was all up to God, this world would have been saved long ago and the rapture would have come. We would all have gone home by now. It's not the will of God that any should perish but that all should come to repentance (**2 Peter 3:9**). If that hasn't happened and it's God's will for it to happen, we have to ask ourselves, why? The reason is that God needs you and me. He's the head; we're the body. We desperately need Jesus, the head. We can't live without Jesus, the head. But he desperately needs His body in order for Him to be able to work on the earth. Think about this, God cannot exercise His authority over the kingdom of darkness in this world unless He does it through the church. He's waiting on us.

That's why He said:

Ephesians 1:22 (NLT) *And God has put all things under the authority of Christ, and he gave him this authority for the benefit of the church.*

Matthew 28:18 (NLT) *Jesus came and told his disciples, "I have been given complete authority in heaven and on earth.*
[19] Therefore, go...

Matthew 18:18 (NKJ) *"Assuredly, I say to you, whatever you bind on earth will be bound in heaven, and whatever you loose on earth will be loosed in heaven."*

With Christ's authority we command circumstances to line up with the will of God. He's waiting for us to command. He's waiting for us to take dominion. He's waiting for us to exercise the authority that He has given us. He's waiting for us to enforce the victory of Calvary. If we don't enforce the victory and the values of Calvary that He died to give us and bring us, it will not happen in our lifetime. We'll never see it. How do we do this? With our words. God gave us the example. He spoke the universe into existence. We are created in His image and likeness. Every word we speak can bring life.

Jesus said in:

John 6:63 (NKJ) *... The words that I speak to you are spirit, and they are life.*

Every **seed** of God, every **word** of God has **all** of His power in it. Not some of His power, **all**. There's not one word that God has spoken that has less power than another, because it's backed up by **all** of God and **all** of His resources. The reason why the word does not work like it should is because of the soil. There are three categories of bad soil and three categories of good soil. The same seed went into all six different soils. In one of the good soils it produced 100-fold return. In the three bad soils it produced no harvest at all.

Everything flourishes in the correct environment. A fish needs water, a duck can swim on top of the water's surface, a cat can climb a tree, a bird can fly, and they all flourish. The seed of God needs its own environment to function — the heart of man that is receptive, treasures and values the seed. When we treasure and value the seed, it will always produce its harvest. It is incorruptible. It can never fail like natural seed can fail.

I believe we are starting to understand the value of God's word, and how to use it to bring God's purposes and plans into existence. We shape our world by planting seeds that we **should** be planting. In **Matthew 13** we learn that Jesus went to Nazareth, His hometown where he grew up as a carpenter's son. Since they knew who He was, they did not accept Him as the Messiah.

> **Matthew 13:57 (NKJ)** *So they were offended at Him. But Jesus said to them, "A prophet is not*

without honor except in his own country and in his own house."

[58] Now He did not do many mighty works there because of their unbelief.

Their lack of faith prevented Jesus from doing signs,
wonders and miracles in His own home town.

Let's read Mark's account of the same incident:

Mark 6:5 (NKJ) *Now He could do no mighty work there, except that He laid His hands on a few sick people and healed them.*

[6] And He marveled because of their unbelief.

Jesus desperately wanted the folks he grew up with in Nazareth to be blessed, to receive healing, miracles and salvations. To overcome the problem of unbelief, He decided to plant seed. He went about the villages in a circuit teaching.

Mark 6:6 (NKJ) *And He marveled because of their unbelief. Then He went about the villages in a circuit, teaching.*

Say this, *"Jesus planted seeds of faith into the hearts of people so they could receive from God."*

The Lord Jesus couldn't do any mighty works in Nazareth. That's why He went teaching, so miracles could come. In other words, He went about sowing seeds that would produce an eventual harvest. But the word had to go out first. Now the Holy Spirit clearly instructs us to do that.

The word must go first. First the seed and then the harvest.

Say this, *"It's impossible for God to do more for me than my words of faith allow Him to do."*

We have to frame our world by the words we speak. The Bible tells us that we are ambassadors for Christ; that we are citizens of heaven; that we are not of this world but we are of heaven, living in this world. What does that mean to us? Let me use an illustration of an ambassador going out from America. We have ambassadors in many countries, in prosperous nations and poverty stricken nations. If an embassy is planted by the United States in a nation that's poverty-stricken, where the people don't even have enough money to put shoes on their feet, never mind own a bicycle, do they tell the ambassador he has to live off the land, that he must live by that land's economy and try and make it? No! They don't. They fence off their property. Then inside the property they plant green grass and trees, and pave the roads. They drive American cars and the ambassador and his staff have all their needs met. They have all the latest hi-tech gadgets brought in from America. Everything they would enjoy in America, they enjoy in the country where they reside as ambassadors. Why? They are ambassadors of the greatest nation in the world. They don't have to live off the economy of that third world country. They live off the economy of America. We are ambassadors of heaven, are we not? So how are we supposed to live in this world? Let's see what Jesus said in:

> **John 17:16 (NKJ)** *they are not of the world, just as I am not of the world.*

The Lord Jesus was praying to the Father for you and for me right here. He says, 'they', so He is talking about us, saying we are not of the world, *"Just as I am not of the world."* Now Jesus is from heaven, right? And we are not of the world just like He's not, because we're of heaven.

> *18 As You sent me into the world, I have also sent them into the world.*

Say this, *"Jesus sent me into the world therefore I am an ambassador of the Lord."*

> **1 Peter 2:11 (NLT)** *Dear brothers and sisters, you are foreigners and aliens here.*

Jesus sent me into the world therefore I am an
ambassador of the Lord.

How are we supposed to live in our role as ambassadors?
Are we supposed to live off this world's economy?

> **Philippians 4:19 (NKJ)** *and my God shall supply*
> *all your need according to His riches in glory by*
> *Christ Jesus.*

It doesn't say, *"He shall sometimes supply our needs accord-ing this world's economy."*

Say this, *"My needs are met by God from* **His** *riches in glory."*

If **Philippians 4:19** said, *"My God shall supply all your need*
by Christ Jesus," that would be wonderful. But he said, "My
God shall supply all your need according to **God's riches**
in glory by Christ Jesus' (**Philippians 4:19**).

Say this, *"I'm living in this world by heaven's economy. I'm not*
limited to the situation I deal with. My words set the stand-
ard by which I will live. I am blessed to be a blessing. **I am**
blessed to be an example of God's generous love*.*
I am a soul-winning machine because I am blessed of God.
Everybody wants to know why I am so blessed, therefore I get
to share my testimony."

Matthew 6:9 (NKJ) *Our Father in heaven, hallowed be Your name.*

[10b] *Your will be done on earth as it is in heaven.*

God wants me to live here like heaven is living. God wants me to live here by heaven's standards, with heaven's joy, heaven's provision, heaven's health, heaven's happiness, heaven's peace, heaven's love. What brings them down? Our words!. As we speak the word of God, as we speak the will of God with boldness and clarity into our circumstances every day, we will begin to create around us the world that our words are saying. The blessings that Jesus paid for at Calvary will be manifest in our lives.

Instead of talking about this world's conditions, let's talk about heaven's abilities. Let's not talk about this world's conditions and lack, let's talk about heaven's abundance in this world of lack and change it.

> Instead of talking about this world's conditions, let's talk about heaven's abilities.

The children of Israel left Egypt and went to Canaan across the wilderness. They moved from slavery to blessing; to the land of milk and honey. Moses sent out twelve spies when they arrived at the border of Canaan. *"Go spy out the land and bring us back a report,"* he told them. Ten of them came back and said, *"We cannot conquer the land because there are* giants there." Two of them, Joshua and Caleb, returned and said, *"We can take the land. God is on our side. Let's go right now."* The three million people believed the ten spies and said, *"We can't go in. There are giants in the land of Canaan."* Who was right and who was wrong? They were both right. They both got what they said. The three million, and the ten spies who doubted, said to Moses, *"Why didn't you let us die in the desert? Why did you bring us here to be killed by the giants?"* They ended up dying in the desert over a 40-year period. Their kids went on and conquered the land with Joshua and Caleb. This is what God says to the Israelites:

> **Numbers 14:28 (NKJ)** *Say to them, 'As I live,'*
> *says the Lord, 'just as you have spoken in My*
> *hearing, so I will do to you:*

So, they all got what they said, exactly what they said. God wanted them to go into Canaan. They said, 'we can't,' and they didn't. Joshua and Caleb said, 'we can,' and they did. Joshua and Caleb took all the children under 40 with them into the Promised Land.

Say this, *"God cannot do more for me than my words of faith allow Him to do."*

Joshua and Caleb framed their world with their words, and they went to live in the land of milk and honey. The other ten spies framed their world with their words. They went back into the wilderness and died in lack.

God cannot do more for me than my words of faith
allow Him to do.

Say this, 'if I am not happy with what I have, I must go farming and plant some seed.'

We must build a land of milk and honey by speaking the word of God. A lifestyle of peace, love and good deeds to mankind is simply a word away. A lifestyle of prosperity, salvation, health and harmony is simply a word away. Let's continue to find out how to release the power of God by speaking His words into our world.

> **Mark 4:26 (NKJ)** *And He said, "The kingdom of God is as if a man should scatter seed on the ground,*
>
> [27] *and should sleep by night and rise by day, and the seed should sprout and grow, he himself does not know how."*

He said the kingdom of God is like a man scattering seed on the ground. It grows and he does not know how. It's a mystery. We had a large mango tree in our garden back Durban, South Africa where I grew up. That mango tree used to produce thousands of mangoes every season. It was huge and laden with mangoes. In 20 years that mango tree must have produced more mangoes than you could put into your house. Now, can you imagine a room full of mangoes? Each one has a seed, capable of producing a mango tree. If you plant a roomful of mango seeds you would have a whole forest of mango trees. Such is the power of an actual seed. Such is the ability of God to create something and put it all in one seed. This seed could fail because it's a natural seed, but you have a Bible and **1 Peter 1:23** says it is filled with incorruptible seeds. It cannot fail. If you plant those seeds they will always produce a harvest. For everything you will need in this life, God has already given you a seed. When you say, *"by Jesus stripes I am healed,"* you plant that seed in your heart. If you stress out, biting your nails, staying up all night, while that seed is germinating and producing a harvest of health in your life, you will still not hurry it on at all. Jesus did not say, *"Plant the seed and then stress out."* He said, *"Plant the seed and go to sleep."* The seed doesn't need your help.

Say this, *"The power to produce a harvest is in the ability of the seed. All I have to do is keep planting and watering my seed."*

How do I plant it? By looking at the scripture and saying, *"By Jesus stripes I am healed."* How do I water it? By saying, *"Praise God I am healed."* I water the seed with my praise and I plant it with my words. The good fight of faith is right there, because the devil is trying to take the seed out of the heart. He doesn't want it to germinate.

So confess, *"By Jesus' stripes I am healed,"* and put it in the heart. **Make sure you act like it is true as far as possible**. Water it a little bit. Say, *"By Jesus' stripes I am healed,"* then praise God and thank Him for it. It won't take long before health, healing and strength begin filling your body, and the only one getting stressed is the devil. So, let us not stress, just let the seed do its work.

Say this, *"I am not going to stress out. I'm going to put my seeds to work. I'm going to put my words to work. I'm not going to struggle and stress. I'm going to say, 'Mr. Giant, this day the Lord will give you into my hands,' and then let the stone go."*

Don't get stressed out. You speak the word and let the seed do its work.

Chapter Five

Reprogramming Our Hearts

You can sit next to a mango tree every day, and every night without sleeping for a week; bite all your nails off and the tree is not going to pay any attention to you. It is going to grow at its own pace whether you stress or sleep, so it is best to sleep by night and rise by day. When problems come in the front door, don't get stressed out and try and deal with it physically. Jesus is saying, 'Just plant the seed.'

When sickness comes in the front door, say, *"by Jesus stripes I am healed."* When poverty comes in the front door, say, *"my God meets all my needs according to His riches in glory by Christ Jesus."* Say the word instead of getting physical about it. Speak to it. Go to sleep and the seed continues to do its work. The word goes into your heart while you are sleeping because your heart (spirit) doesn't sleep. When you wake up, you discover there's a harvest there. And you think, 'How did that happen?' We don't know how the seed works, but it works. I can't figure out how there could be an entire mango tree and 10,000 mangoes in one mango seed. I can't figure that out. You plant those mangoes and you have a forest all in one mango seed. No scientist can make one of these, as smart as they are. Yet those scientists will tell me this happened when the Big Bang took place in the middle of nowhere and that suddenly there were trillions of seeds. Can you imagine going right back to the day of creation? Think of all those original seeds. They carried every single fruit tree we see today, every vegetable we see today, and they keep reproducing. They were all in those original seeds. We can't figure that out and scientists can't recreate it. But they say we came from monkeys. We were all monkeys at one time. You know, when I hear a scientist talking like that I think, 'Yeah, looking at you, and listening to you, I am beginning to think you are right. **You** came from a monkey, that's for sure. I am beginning to believe it.' How they can be that dumb and still breathe, I don't know. I think some of these scientists are the eighth wonder of the world. Now, then Jesus said in:

> **Mark 4:28 (NKJ)** *For the earth yields crops by itself: first the blade, then the head, after that the full grain in the head.*
>
> [29] *But when the grain ripens, immediately he puts in the sickle, because the harvest has come."*

It takes time. It grows little by little. What is He saying? The same thing He said earlier in the chapter. Remember this, Jesus spoke about the seed being planted in six different soils in **Mark 4: wayside** soil, **stony** soil, **rocky** soil and three categories of **good** soil. The same seed went into all six different soils. The seed could **not** produce in three categories and it **could** produce 30, 60, and 100 in the good category. Why? The condition of the soil determines the quality of the harvest.

Say this, *"My heart determines how well God's word will work in my life."*

If I have a problem with my faith, it is not the fault of the seed. The fault is in the heart. I need to figure out what's wrong in there. Either I'm not paying attention to the word, or I don't value the word; I don't care about it — or I am not meditating in it. I don't think it's important so I'm neglecting it, and I'm listening to many things I shouldn't, and they are going into my heart and choking the word.

My heart determines how well God's word will work
in my life.

People can say, *"You're no good. You'll never make it. You're a failure. You're going to be poor the rest of your life. You'll never get healed."* Don't listen to that. Jesus said, 'take heed **what** you hear and take heed **how** you hear.' Let's have enough sense to know we are protecting and taking care of our heart, our garden, because it needs to produce the harvest for us.

> [29] *But when the grain ripens, immediately he puts in the sickle, because the harvest has come."*

Does God put in the sickle or does the man who sowed the seed put in the sickle? The man does.

Say this, *"When I become fully persuaded, I put in the sickle."* Now how do I do that? The same way I planted.

Say this, *"By Jesus stripes I **am** healed."*

Say this, *"I **am** prospering. I have the money to do what I need to do."*

Say this, *"I **am** a soul winner. Fred Bloggs **will** be saved."*

Say this, *"Fred Bloggs I see you saved."*

By doing this we become fully persuaded and the harvest comes in (**Romans 4:21**).

> **Romans 4:21 (NKJ)** *and being **fully convinced** that what He had promised He was also able to perform.*

> **Matthew 12:35 (NKJ)** *A good man out of the good treasure of his heart brings forth good things, and an evil man out of the evil treasure brings forth evil things.*

Very often we fail to receive because our patience runs out. We need to continue confessing the promise, *"by Jesus stripes I am healed,"* praise Him, **act well**, and don't give up on our patience. We understand we are applying faith. But faith grows in the heart, first the blade, then the shoot, then the ear, then the corn.

A good seed to sow for prosperity is:

> **Luke 6:38 (NKJ)** *Give, and it will be given to you:*
> *good measure, pressed down, shaken together, and*
> *running over will be put into your bosom. For with*
> *the same measure that you use, it will be measured*
> *back to you."*

You can say, *"Praise God I have given therefore it is given to back me good measure, pressed down, shaken together and running over. I receive it now, in Jesus' name."*

> **Luke 17:5 (NKJ)** *And the apostles said to the Lord,*
> *"Increase our faith."*

This is important. The Lord Jesus is talking with the disciples and they say to Him, *"Lord, Increase our faith."* The disciples asked Him how to increase their faith, therefore He will not tell them something that has nothing to do with their question. He will answer the question.

> **Luke 17: 6 (NKJ)** *So the Lord said, "**If** you have*
> *faith as a **mustard seed**, you can say to this*
> *mulberry tree, 'Be pulled up by the roots and be*
> *planted in the sea,' and it would obey you.*

Take your pen and circle the word '**if**' in your Bible. This is conditional. If you have faith as a mustard seed, you can say. If you do not have faith as a mustard seed you can't say. What He is telling us is that faith works like a seed works.

Say that, *"faith works like a seed works."*

'If you have faith as a mustard seed.' How does a seed work? You take the seed, you plant it in the ground, you give it a little water now and again, and it grows. You don't have to pay attention to it more than that. Just make sure you don't put anything on top of it. Faith works like that. How? I say, *"By Jesus stripes I am healed."* I read the verse, look at it, and as I do that, the seed goes through my ear and into my heart. In the seed is the power to produce healing. It comes alive in me and produces health in me. In other words, if I have the verse, I have the seed and the faith to move the mulberry tree. Faith comes by hearing God's word, and faith comes by the seed. God could have said this, *"If you have the word, (the promise), in your heart, you could say to the mulberry tree, 'move into the sea' and it would obey you."* And it would obey whom? You or God? Why would it obey you? Because you are the one giving the instruction. It's the faith in the seed doing the work, not you. The seed is producing the healing, the seed is producing the prosperity, out of the good soil of your heart. The soil of your heart allows the seed to produce.

If we have the promise in our heart we can say and it will work. Now some folks want to get a thousand scriptures before they feel they've got it. They are gathering hoards of scriptures like a squirrel collecting nuts. That is not necessary. Imagine trying to put 100 healing scriptures into your heart. That will take a long time. It will take 100 times longer than it would take to get one healing scripture into your heart. One verse will do the job. Every verse has all of God's power in it. It's not the amount of scripture we collect that matters. It's how much time we meditate on any one scripture that matters. Between one and ten scriptures should be enough. The Lord Jesus didn't say, 'if you have faith like a bag full of mustard seeds.' He's telling you one tiny mustard seed is sufficient. Now how big is a mustard seed? A mustard seed is one of the smallest seeds on the earth. He didn't say, 'If you have faith like an avocado seed.' So then we understand that the principle of faith is the same as the principle of seeds.

Say this, *"faith works like planting seeds. Faith works like seeds work."*

Say this, *"My words spoken are seeds. The seed has within itself the creative energy of God."*

Now say this, 'If I have the seed in my heart, I have the faith to move the mulberry tree. If I have the seed, I have the faith, to move the problem in my life.'

> **Hebrews 11:1 (NKJ)** *Now faith is the substance of things hoped for, the evidence of things not seen.*

The Bible said faith is the substance of things hoped for, so you could say that the seed is the substance of things hoped for. What is substance? Substance is something material.

Say that, *"The seed, God's word, is the substance of things I hope for."*

The thing you want is in the spirit realm, because everything comes from God, who is a spirit. **Therefore God has given us the seed, which is the substance of the thing we can't see**.

> The seed, God's word, is the substance of things I hope for.

Faith is the substance of the thing I hope for, the evidence of things not seen. God's healing verse is the substance, the evidence that I am healed, while I am still sick. God's prosperity verse is the evidence that I am prospering, while I am still in lack. Any verse I find that meets my need becomes the evidence that I have it, even though I can't see it yet.

For example, if you need mango trees and I hand you a whole bunch of mango seeds I have solved your problem. Well, God's done that. We can hold our Bible up and say, *"Everything I ever need God has given me seeds for. It's in my Bible."*

> The seed is our evidence that we have what we want from God. Just plant it.

Don't dig up your seed. God said, *"Hold fast to your confession of faith without wavering,"* which means, when we say, *"By Jesus' stripes I **am** healed,"* don't go and change it the next day and say, *"I thought I was,"* or *"Maybe I am."* If you say, *"I am prospering,"* don't go the next day and say, *"How am I going to pay these bills?"*

Another thing, if you say, *"I'm prospering,"* and it doesn't come in a month, don't get paranoid. Keep saying, *"I'm prospering."* If you say, *"I'm a soul winner, I win souls everywhere I go,"* and if you don't win one for a month, don't panic. Keep saying it, God will change you, or fix you to make you into a soul winner.

I'll illustrate with a little story about two friends of mine, Joe Soap and Fred Bloggs. They're fictitious friends of mine, and they've helped me many times. They both are farmers today and there's a fence between the two farms. Fred Bloggs has a beautiful harvest and as he's driving down his farm road, he's singing, *"Oh what a beautiful morning. Oh what a wonderful day. Oh what a wonderful feeling everything's going my way."* And he's just so happy. He drives past Joe Soap's farm and he looks over the fence and he sees a dust cloud in the middle of nowhere. As he draws closer, he sees Joe Soap lying in the dust, beating his fists on the ground, crying out loud in bitter sorrow and anguish. Fred Bloggs pulls up his jeep and says, *"Joe Soap, what a wonderful morning. What a wonderful day. What a wonderful feeling everything's going my way. Why cryest thou?"*

And Joe Soap says, *"Can you believe it? I've planted tons of seeds in thousands of acres and not one has grown. Not one."* Fred Bloggs says, *"This is amazing. When did you plant these seeds?"*

Joe replies, *"Yesterday."*

Here's the problem family — yesterday is too soon. The Bible said seed time and harvest. The Bible didn't say seed and harvest. It said seed **time** and harvest. We live in a world where everything is instant. We have instant coffee, instant nails, instant hair, instant microwave and so on. We need to understand, there's time needed for the harvest.

> **Ephesians 1:13 (NKJ)** *In Him (Christ) you also trusted, after you heard the word of truth, the gospel of your salvation; in whom also, having believed, you were sealed with the Holy Spirit of promise,*

Say this, 'I'm born again by receiving the seed, God's word. God's word carries God's life, which was deposited into my heart. When I heard the word I received my salvation.'

> **John 6:63 (NKJ)** *It is the Spirit who gives life . . . the words that I speak to you are spirit, and they are life.*

See again, God's word carries life.

> **John 3:6 (NKJ)** *That which is born of the flesh is flesh, and that which is born of the Spirit is spirit.*

So you are born again by the spirit of God, which is contained in the seed.

> **1 John 3:9 (NKJ)** *Whoever has been born of God does not sin, for His seed remains in him; and he cannot sin, because he has been born of God.*

> **John 5:24 (NKJ)** *Most assuredly, I say to you, he who hears My word and believes in Him who sent Me has everlasting life, and shall not come into judgment, but has passed from death into life.*

Say this, *"I have passed from death into life because I received the word which I heard."*

> **Genesis 1:11 (NKJ)** *Then God said, "Let the earth bring forth grass, the herb that yields seed, and the fruit tree that yields fruit according to its kind, whose seed is in itself, on the earth"; and it was so.*

Everything around us works by seeds which brings us right back to,

> **Mark 4:26 (NKJ)** *The kingdom of God is as if a man should scatter seed on the ground.*

Say this, *"I understand the vastness of seed time and harvest. The entire kingdom of God works by seeds. Therefore, I need to speak words of God, allow them to go into my heart and reprogram my heart because it will produce whatever I put in it. Just like soil will grow the good and the bad. My heart will produce the good things in my life and the bad things."*

Therefore I now program my heart, and say to myself, 'I am blessed of God. God favors me. Wherever I go I am blessed and highly favored. Everything I do prospers. I am healed by Jesus' stripes and I live in divine health. I hear God's voice and I know His voice and I follow Him. I am walking in God's perfect plan for my life. I'm blessed in the city, blessed in the field. My storehouse is blessed. My home is blessed. My children are blessed. My parents are blessed. Everyone around me is blessed because I am blessed with overflowing blessing. I'm blessed to be a blessing. Praise God, nothing takes me by surprise. God always warns me; wherever I go, the road ahead of me is prepared. Things are in order for my arrival. I always get placed in the front of the line. Wherever I go I get the good deals. The opportunities of life always come my way. I am more than an overcomer. I am more than a conqueror. In all these things Christ has already won the victory for me. Praise God."

"God keeps me holy.
God keeps me faithful.
God keeps my motives pure.
I am continually receiving the knowledge of God's will, in all wisdom and spiritual understanding, that I might fully please the Father in all things" (**Colossians 1:9**).

Chapter Six

Positive Or Negative?

Understanding the power of positive confession will make a positive impact on our entire life. Every area of our life will improve — spiritually, physically, mentally, financially, family, and relationships.

> **Luke 17:6 (NKJ)** *So the Lord said, "If you have faith as a mustard seed, you can say to this mulberry tree, 'Be pulled up by the roots and be planted in the sea,' and it would obey you."*

We learnt that faith works like a seed. A seed is planted, it germinates, and it produces a harvest. The seed is the word. When we have the word we have the seed. When we have the seed and the word in the heart we have the faith to move the mulberry tree. Why? Because the faith to move the mulberry tree is in the word, it is in the seed. When a problem comes my way, I have to say what the word says to the problem. First I need to find out what the word says about my problem. I take that scripture, read it a few times, meditate on it, get it into my heart and then speak to the problem. **Jesus said you've got to release the faith in the seed by saying something**. He said, *"if you have faith as a mustard seed you can say,"* so faith is released by saying.

Now with that in mind, go to:

> **Mark 11:23 (NKJ)** *For **assuredly**, I say to you,*
> *whoever says to this mountain, 'Be removed and be*
> *cast into the sea,' and does not doubt in his heart, but*
> *believes that those things he says will be done, he will*
> *have whatever he says.*

I know you've seen this a thousand times but look at it again. In the New King James Jesus said, "**Assuredly** *I say to you.*" He doesn't have to say that. Jesus could have simply said, "*I say to you,*" that would be enough. This has to be very important.

> **Mark 11:23 (NKJ)** *For **assuredly**, I say to you,*
> *whoever says to this mountain...*

He's standing on the Mount of Olives between Bethany and Jerusalem.

> **Mark 11:23 (NKJ)** *...be removed and be cast*
> *into the sea and does not doubt in his heart, but*
> *believes that those things he says (will come), will be*
> *done, he will have whatever he says.*

The Lord Jesus said whoever says, will have whatever he says, if he believes in his heart what he says.

Now say this, *"That is talking about me. I have whatever I say if I believe what I say."*

That means if I say bad things, I'm going to get bad things. If I say good things, I'm going to get good things. I have a question. Is Jesus saying that this law of releasing faith works by saying? Is that all there is to it? No, what else is it? You must believe in your heart. Saying won't work without believing, and believing won't work without saying. How many of us believe God's word is true? That's half of the problem solved. How many of us can add our confession to what we believe in the word being true? We can all do this. How many of us believe by Jesus' stripes we were healed? So when we say that we are believing and saying. Somebody asked, *"Pastor Theo, is this all necessary? Do we have to spend all this time waffling on about confession? Do we have to spend all this time talking about the power of positive confession?"* With this in mind let's go to:

> **Romans 10:9 (NKJ)** *That **IF** you confess with your mouth the Lord Jesus **AND** believe in your heart that God has raised Him from the dead, you will be saved.*

Notice the word **if**. It means if you don't confess with your mouth, this doesn't work. You have to confess with your mouth, **and** believe in your heart. In order to be saved you have to say with your mouth Jesus is Lord, and **believe** in your heart that God raised Him from the dead.

> [10] *For with the heart one believes unto righteousness, and with the mouth confession is made unto salvation.*

"With the mouth confession is made unto salvation," or you could say confession is made into the salvation experience. You enter into the salvation experience by saying with your mouth, *"Jesus is Lord,"* and you believe He's risen from the dead. A good example of the power of positive confession is the story of Moses leading the children of Israel out of Egypt into the promised land of Canaan. After 400 years of being slaves in Egypt, the children of Israel left and finally arrived at the border of Canaan. Moses selected one leader from each of the twelve tribes of Israel and said, *"Go in and spy out the land of Canaan so we can plan our battle strategy to conquer the land."* The twelve spies came back with a report about the great big fruit and grapes and so on. Ten had a negative report and two had a positive report.

> **Numbers 13:25 (NKJ)** *And they returned from spying out the land after forty days.*
>
> *[26] Now they departed and came back to Moses and Aaron and all the congregation of the children of Israel in the Wilderness of Paran, at Kadesh; they brought back word to them and to all the congregation, and showed them the fruit of the land.*
>
> *[27] Then they told him, and said: "We went to the land where you sent us. It truly flows with milk and honey, and this is its fruit.*
>
> *[28] Nevertheless the people who dwell in the land are strong; the cities are fortified and very large; moreover we saw the descendants of Anak there."*

The children of Israel knew exactly who the descendants of Anak were. They knew they were giants. When they heard that the cities were very large and fortified they panicked. They started crying out loud, *"We've walked all this way, we've waited 400 years to get here and now we have to face giants?"*

> *30 Then Caleb quieted the people before Moses, and said, "Let us go up at once and take possession, for we are well able to overcome it."*

So Caleb calmed them down, they all thought, *"Okay, maybe."* And then they looked to the ten spies to see if they were in agreement with this.

> *31 But the men who had gone up with him said, "We are not able to go up against the people, for they are stronger than we."*

And three million Israelites freaked out.

I would like you to notice these two confessions of faith. Joshua and Caleb had a confession of faith that said, *"We can go up and take the land."* A confession from the other ten was also a confession of faith. *"We cannot go up to take the land for they are stronger than we."* Notice those two confessions, two completely opposing confessions. Both of those parties believed what they were saying was true.

> **Numbers 13:32 (NKJ)** *And they gave the children of Israel a bad report of the land which they had spied out, saying, "The land through which we have gone as*

> *spies is a land that devours its inhabitants, and all the*
> *people whom we saw in it are men of great stature.*

The Old King James says, "**an evil report**."

Say this, *"a negative report is an evil report."*

If you say, *"I'm sick, I'm poor. We are getting divorced; my children are up to no good. Sorry, we just don't have the money to do it under the circumstances,"* then you have given a negative report with your words. Why are you under the circumstances? You're supposed to be on top. Why do you place yourself under the circumstances? Do you say, *"The circumstances control my life. They made me do this. I'm just a helpless victim. If this didn't happen in my life I wouldn't be such a dummy. If my teacher didn't say that to me when I was three years old, or five years old, or nine years old, I wouldn't be in the mess that I'm in today. Woe is me."* That is all an evil report. God says that is evil. You are sinning when you say things like that. God is on our side and we do not have to tolerate all that defeat and nonsense.

> [32] *And they gave the children of Israel a bad report of the land which they had spied out, saying, "The land through which we have gone as spies is a land that devours its inhabitants, and all the people whom we saw in it are men of great stature.*
>
> [33] *There we saw the giants (the descendants of Anak came from the giants); and we were like grasshoppers in our own sight, and so we were in their sight."*

They must have looked at each other and looked at the giants and thought, *"You know what? You look like a grasshopper next to this 13-foot man over there."* Then they said, *"Let's just hop out of here."* They had this image of themselves but did they stop and say, *"Excuse me Mister giant, what do I look like to you?"*

"Oh, you look like a grasshopper, sonny."

"Just as I thought."

I don't think so. How did they know what the giants were thinking?

Say this, *"If I have a bad image of myself, I think everybody else thinks that way about me. What I think about me, I think others think about me. Therefore, I need to see me as God sees me. God sees me loved, blessed, highly favored."*

You see when they said, *"We are grasshoppers,"* they were accepting total defeat. That would be like saying, *"under the circumstances I could do nothing."* That is a death confession. We might think, 'Poor people, they should never have done that.' But we might be doing something similar. It's interesting to note that they saw themselves as grasshoppers and:

> **Proverbs 23:7** *says, "as a man thinks in his heart, so is he."*

This means, the minute I agree to that image of me, the minute I agree to me being without anything in life, that's how I am. The minute I agree to me being sick and never

ever getting well, that's how I am. The minute I see myself with a family scattered everywhere, that's how I'll be. The minute I see myself being unpopular and disliked everywhere, that's how I am.

Do you see that? That's what we just read. That's what happened with these grasshopper mentality people. They had this image of themselves and they conquered themselves. We are not to do that. I'm not saying that we should be bold in our own arrogance. I'm not suggesting for a moment that we should be bold in our fleshly strength. I'm not saying that we should have faith in ourselves. We should have faith in God because He is with us and the Bible tells us He will never fail us.

> **Ephesians 6:10 (NKJ)** *Finally, my brethren, be strong in the Lord and in the power of His might.*

Now, that didn't mean, *"Go down to the gym, work out, and get strong."* It didn't say, *"Put your chin up, put your shoulders back, you sloppy thing. Try again. Charge up that mountain one more time."* It said, *"Be strong in the Lord and the power of the Lord's might."*

Say this, *"I must be strong with God's strength, not my strength."* Did Paul say, *"I can do all things through **my** own strength."*? **No**. He said, "I can do all things **through Christ** who strengthens me." (**Philippians 4:13**)

> **Psalm 27:1 (NKJ)** ...*the Lord is the strength of my life.*

We've got to be bold because Christ is our strength.

> **1 John 4:4 (NKJ)** *You are of God, little children, and have overcome them, because He who is in you is greater than he who is in the world.*

Say this, "*God is in me and if He's on my side I'm on the winning team.*" We can add, "*God is with me therefore I will overcome this sickness. God is with me therefore I will overcome this financial problem. God is with me therefore I will win my family to Jesus. God is with me therefore I am a soul winner. God is with me therefore I can overcome the giants of life, the problems I face. I will overcome every problem, not some of them.*"

Now you have to keep making these confessions until you get bold and say them confidently. Some people say them as if they are not sure they will work. The devil can hear that. He can hear you're not sure about yourself. Even if your knees are shaking, say it boldly. The devil can't see your heart. He doesn't know if you're shivering in your boots.

> **Numbers 14:1 (NKJ)** *So all the congregation lifted up their voices and cried, and the people wept that night.*
>
> ² *And all the children of Israel complained against Moses and Aaron...*

"All the children of Israel complained..." Not some, all. Look how it went, like a bushfire in a dry forest. **Three million people contaminated with doubt, unbelief and fear, in a few moments**. Isn't that incredible? **They accepted their own death in a second, in a heartbeat.** Listen to this positive confession of faith:

> *2...if only we had died in the land of Egypt. Or if only we had died in this wilderness.*

"I don't want to die by the giants, I'd rather starve and die with no water in the desert. But don't let the giants kill me in Canaan. If only, and this is my greatest dream, if only I'd died in the desert. If only I could have stayed in Egypt and been a slave. If only I could be whipped every day."

Isn't it amazing? In South Africa we call people like that mielie-mouthed. 'Mielie' is an Afrikaans word for corn. They have such a wide mouth from complaining, they can put the whole corncob into their mouth sideways. Something goes wrong and they just want to go back into the world, and say, *"I'm not going back to church again."* Or, *"I guess I'll stay sick for the rest of my life. I guess I'll just stay poor for the rest of my life. I guess no one likes me and nothing good will ever happen to me, nothing good will ever come my way. You see I told you so. It's bad now but it's going to get worse tomorrow."*

> *4 So they said to one another, "Let us select a leader and return to Egypt."*

> [5] *Then Moses and Aaron fell on their faces before all the assembly of the congregation of the children of Israel.*
>
> [6] *But Joshua the son of Nun and Caleb the son of Jephunneh, who were among those that spied out the land, tore their clothes ;*
>
> [7] *and they spoke to the congregation of the children of Israel saying: "The land we passed through to spy out is an exceedingly good land.*
>
> [8] *If the Lord delights in us, then He will bring us into this land and give it to us, 'a land which flows with milk and honey.'*
>
> [9] *Only do not* **rebel** *against the Lord, nor* **fear** *the people of the land, for they are our bread; their protection has departed from them, and the Lord is with us. Do not fear them."*

Say this, **"Confessing doubt and unbelief is rebellion."** Note, the word says, *"only do not* **rebel** *against the Lord, do not fear the people of the land."* Now watch this. *"For they are our bread."* We're going to eat them up. *"Their protection has departed from them and the Lord is with us. Do not fear them."*

Confessing doubt and unbelief is rebellion.

And all the congregation said, *"Praise the Lord. Let's go on."* **Not at all**.

> [10] *And all the congregation said to stone them with*
> *stones.*

Say this, *"I must not be surprised if very few people agree with my confession of faith."*

Joshua and Caleb were the only two that were in faith. They believed they could go forward. Three million people along with the ten spies did not believe it.

Say this, "My Canaan is every promise in the Bible. Everything Jesus bought at Calvary is my Canaan. I can enter my Canaan and come out of my circumstances. I can cross from Egypt to Canaan by the words of my mouth. I must not fear the future. I must not fear laying hold of the blessings. I must not fear laying hold of health and prosperity, a happy family and being used by God. I must not fear my future, whatever God has, however big it is, I know He is well able to take me through. I will succeed because God is on my side. I am like Joshua and Caleb. I am a winner. I'm an overcomer. **I'm a giant slayer**. In the name of Jesus, I'm not going back to Egypt. I'm going on to Canaan. Whatever God has for me I'm going to walk in it.'

It will happen by boldly confessing the promise of God. We will not get there any other way. Two people out of three million had faith. Can you see the odds? It's not surprising today that so few are willing to take this route and go this way, the way of Joshua and Caleb. I'm a Joshua and a Caleb follower, are you? Ten spies said they couldn't conquer the land and Joshua and Caleb said they could. Who was right?

Joshua and Caleb, or the ten spies? They are **both** right. They **both** said and they **both** got what they said. While Joshua, Caleb and all the children of all those doubters, were taking possession of their inheritance in Canaan, the ten doubting spies and all those doubting older Israelites, were already dead and buried in the desert.

> **Numbers 14:26 (NKJ)** *And the Lord spoke to Moses and Aaron, saying,*
>
> [27] *"How long shall I bear with this evil congregation who complain against Me? I have heard the complaints which the children of Israel make against Me.*
>
> [28] *Say to them, 'As I live,' says the Lord, 'just as you have spoken in My hearing, so I will do to you:*

When God says, *"As I live,' says the Lord,"* we'd better know this is serious stuff. He's not playing games. He means business. Very few times did God ever say this in the Bible. What He is going to say now, to me, is like, **"Assuredly** *I say to you,"* from **Mark 11:23**. Both of these serious situations deal with confession. Can we understand how important positive confession is to God?

> [28] *Say to them, 'As I live,' says the Lord, 'just as you have spoken in My hearing, so I will do to you:'*

Those who say they can't, are right. Those who say they can, are right. That's what God said here in **Numbers 14:28**. He said, *"Just as I live..."* In the New Testament Jesus said,

"Assuredly, I say to you..." Both of those statements revolve around words of faith.

Say this, *"it's obvious what I say is important to God, and it is important to my life."*

People have approached me and said, *"Pastor Theo, there is the Job issue. You can't argue about that. Job suffered, and I am just like Job. That's all there is to it, I'm like a modern-day Job. God is molding me. He is fixing me and improving me. That's why I have suffered all these calamities, sickness and problems throughout my life."*

> What I say is important to God, and it is important to my life.

I don't know why those folk go to a doctor or hospital, and get everyone fighting God with them. If they think they're supposed to be sick, why get everyone involved in their sin of fighting God, trying to get well? Just submit to the sickness and die! Learn whatever it is you're supposed to learn. Job wasn't suffering because God wanted him to suffer.

> **Job 3:25 (NKJ)** *For the thing I greatly feared is come upon me. And what I dreaded has happened to me.*
>
> *26 I have no rest for trouble comes.*

Job said these words to his friends, *"The thing I greatly feared is come upon me,"* and then he said, *"I have no rest for trouble comes."* We can see that Job brought this on himself with his confessions. Let us not confess our fears. **It's not the giants in life that defeat us; it's what we say about the giants in life that defeat us.** It's not the problems of life that defeat us; it's what we say about them that either defeat us or put us over.

It is important for us not to confess for something when we don't know what God's will is on the matter. We **do** know healing is for us. Financial prosperity is for us, so we can believe God for these things. We can believe for harmony and blessing in our home. We can exercise our God-given authority etc.

> It's not the problems of life that defeat us; it is what we say about them that either defeat us or put us over.

We don't know what God's will is for our future. It would not be wise to confess, *"I am going to be a missionary in China,"* if you haven't asked God about it. Or, *"I am going to live in such-and-such a city."* We need to be led by the Spirit concerning our future, and then confess what God's will is. Far too many Christians suffer lack because they are geographically out of God's will, and it will not improve until they start following the cloud. You can order my message titled, '**The Cloud Is Moving**', from Celebration 2013 in Johannesburg.

Tell people, *"I believe I know God's plan for my life."* Or confess **Colossians 1:9**. Not many days will pass before something will start growing on the inside of you, and you'll start to know what you're supposed to be doing.

We have to be careful. We don't want to use this faith message incorrectly. Anything the Bible says is ours we can believe for right away. But if we don't know God's plan, let's believe for it before we start confessing.

> **Mark 4:24 (NKJ)** *Then He said to them, "Take heed what you hear. With the same measure you use, it will be measured to you; and to you who hear, more will be given."*

Let's have a look at that word '**what**'. Take heed **what** you hear. What does that mean? That means that we should not just listen to anything. It means be discerning. It means be selective in what you hear. Wouldn't it be good if the children of Israel could have heard that sermon from Jesus before the twelve spies returned from spying out the land? If Jesus was there and preached that sermon, and said, *"take heed what you hear, the twelve spies are coming back."* They would have listened to Joshua and Caleb, and would have said to the ten spies, *"Uh-uh. We don't agree with you guys. Jesus said, 'take heed what you hear,' I'm not going to* *listen to this. Don't talk to me. I don't want to hear that doubt and unbelief stuff. God has already said 'I've given you the land.' God has already said 'every place that your foot treads on I've given to you.' I'm sorry I don't want to hear that doubt. I'm going with Joshua and Caleb."*

Say this, *"I must not listen to people who say I can't, people who say it will never happen for me, people who say I'll never be well again, people who say I'll never amount to anything, people who say, I'll never succeed in this business, people who say business is tough. I must not listen to that."*

> **Mark 4:24 (NKJ)** *Then He said to them, 'Take heed what you hear. With the same measure you use, it will be measured to you; and to you who hear, more will be given.'*

That means **the way** we listen, or, in proportion **to how we listen**, that's the proportion we will receive. To you who hear, more will be given.

Say this, *"***I receive by hearing***. When I listen to God's word, I listen to faith. I receive more blessing from God. The more I meditate on God's word, the more blessed I become."*

> **Luke 8:18 (NKJ)** *Therefore **take heed how you hear**. For whoever has, **to him more will be given**; and whoever does not have, even what he seems to have will be taken from him.*

In **Mark**, Jesus said, *"Take heed **what** you hear."* Here He says, *"Take heed **how** you hear."* The two are different. Take heed **how** you hear means you know what you're supposed to listen to and you're supposed to give it your full attention. Why?

[18] For whoever has, to him more will be given.

So we see it comes by hearing, and whoever does not have, even what he seems to have, will be taken away. Jesus said there are some that don't have anything but it seems like they do. For example, unsaved people. Jesus said, *"What does it help if you gain the whole world and lose your soul and go to hell?"* You leave it all behind and you burn in hell for eternity with nothing. What does it help you if you gain the whole world and lose your soul and go to hell?

We know that Christians also have things in this life that they never received by this principle. The enemy takes some of our things from us, perhaps our health, possibly our finances, maybe our families; whatever it might be. If we don't hear properly, if we don't understand what we are doing, **what** we are saying, what God is saying, the devil can take it. But since we are hearing and finding out **how** to use our faith, the devil will not be able to take it from us.

Ignorance is our greatest enemy, not the devil.

Say this, *"What we keep and what we lose is dependent on* **how** *we hear and* **what** *we hear."*

We are starting to find out that everything in this life depends on **how** we hear and **what** we hear. Whatever we **lose** and whatever we **keep** depends on **how** we hear and **what** we hear, because it gets into the heart and the heart will produce the harvest. **If it doesn't get into the heart, the devil can steal it**.

> What we keep and what we lose is dependent on
> how we hear, and what we hear.

Say this, *"I know the word. Satan will not steal anything from me. I'm moving on, I'm moving forward. Praise God I'm making progress. God is on my side. I'm an overcomer. I'm not ignorant of the devil's devices. He will not steal the word from me.* **I understand the word of God is the source of my victory**. *I declare in the name of Jesus I hear the word, I listen to the word, It is a treasure to me, it is valuable to me. I take heed to it. It gets into my heart and when I speak it, the mountain moves."*

Chapter Seven

Guarding Our Hearts

Proverbs 4:23 (NIV) *Above all else, guard your heart, for it is the wellspring of life.*

When God says, **"above all else,"** He is essentially saying, 'this is the most important thing we have to take care of.' That means we have to take care of this more than our spouse, our children, our money, our business, or anything else. If we understand the reason for it, we will see that when we take care of our heart that we **are** taking care of our spouse, our family, and our business. If we neglect our heart we will see that we are neglecting our spouse, our family, our business, and everything else, because everything is blessed through our heart. The Bible says, *"for it affects* **everything** *you do."* God's blessings come to us through God's word, entering our heart, then into the natural physical world.

> [24] *Avoid all perverse talk. Stay far from corrupt speech.*

We want to stay away from talking strife, division, doubt, unbelief, fear, or anything negative. We do not want to be involved in it, or give our ear to it. We don't want to hear it because it gets into the heart, and it contaminates the production factory of our life. Everything we receive from

God must come from the Word by faith, into the heart, and out of the mouth, into the natural. There's no other way for it to happen. Whatever we receive from God comes via the heart before it comes into the natural. Therefore, we don't want to corrupt the process by listening to things that are not going to help us, but hinder us.

For example, one night in 1979, while in my car, I heard the Lord say, *"Go to Bedfordview and start a church."* That is a suburb of Johannesburg. I accepted that word from God, shared it with my wife, and she also accepted it. We meditated on it and discussed it between ourselves, and then we discussed it with our close friends. Friends of like precious faith. There are some folks you can't share everything with because they might mock you, or laugh at you, or joke with you, and you don't want that to get into your heart, especially when you're meditating on something God has given you. As we spoke about it, God gave us more revelation, and we declared that revelation. We discussed what kind of church it would be, the impact it would have, how God would work in that church, and many different aspects of that future ministry. Today the physical manifestation of that revelation is standing in Johannesburg and it is doing exactly what we said it would, back in February 1979.

A similar thing happened in 1992, when I received a night vision from the Lord and a word from God, regarding planting a church in San Antonio. I shared it with my wife, she accepted the word from the Lord, and we began to minister to each other and to certain people about what God was going to do in San Antonio. Today you see part of that in the natural. There is a lot more that God told us is going to happen that is still to come. It's in the heart. So what we have are two ministries that were at one time a word in the heart. The big picture is to plant 1,000 churches from our sons, and establish 50 to 100 Bible Schools, teaching the word of God around the world.

1 Peter 1:23 tells us that **God's word is seed**. **Luke 8** and **Mark 4** tell us **God's word is seed**. Therefore we receive the **word** or a **seed** in the heart and it germinates and brings forth fruit after its kind into our lives. How does that happen?

> ***Matthew 12:35 (NKJ)*** *A good man out of the good treasure of his heart brings forth good things, and an evil man out of the evil treasure brings forth evil things.*

At one time these two churches were in my heart and Bev's heart and now they're in the natural.

All of us have a destiny from God. All of us were created for a purpose. Just look out your windows and see the multitudes of thousands, and in fact billions of people who do not know Jesus, who are headed for an eternity in the flames of hell. Each believer has a call, a destiny, and it revolves primarily around us working as a team to bring in the lost harvest of souls.

Ephesians 2:10 (NIV) *For we are God's workmanship, created in Christ Jesus* **to do good works**, *which* **God prepared** *in advance for us to do.*

Ephesians 1:11 (NIV) *In Christ we were also chosen, having been predestined* **according to the plan of God** *who works out everything in conformity* **with the purpose of his will**.

1 Corinthians 3:5 (NIV) *What, after all, is Apollos? And what is Paul? Only servants, through whom you came to believe -* **as the Lord has assigned to each his task**.

Ecclesiastes 6:10 (NLT) *Everything has already been decided. It was known long ago what each person would be.* **So there's no use arguing with God about your destiny**.

You have a destiny, a purpose, and a plan from God, assigned just to you, custom built. If you don't know what it is, you can solve that problem very quickly.

Say this, *"I believe I know God's plan for my life."* Or you can confess **Colossians 1:9**. As you keep saying that, it will come alive in you, and within a few days you will know what it is you must do. Why? God's desperate for you to know. There are lives in the balance. God wants you to know far more than you ever want to know. **Get involved in your local church — start there**.

Jesus said, *"My sheep hear my voice and I know them and they follow me"* (**John 10:27**). If Jesus said you know His voice, I guess He knows what He is talking about, don't you? If you can pray in tongues, it will make it **far** easier to receive God's guidance.

> **1 Corinthians 2:14 (NKJ)** ...*the things of the Spirit of God...are spiritually* **discerned**.

> **Isaiah 50:4 (NLT)** *Morning by morning He awakens me and opens my understanding to his will.*

Now is the time. When we get to heaven and time comes for us to receive our rewards from Jesus, we want to hear, 'Well done good and faithful servant.' If at this point, when we stand before Jesus, and we are not happy with what we have done for our King, we cannot come back to earth and lay up more treasure. Our opportunity will be over. Whatever we have done we will be rewarded for, and whatever we have not done, we will **not** be rewarded for. Our destiny, our purpose, must be fulfilled at that moment. It's not going to happen without faith. It's not going to happen without speaking it.

Let's say this, 'Only when I boldly confess then and then only do I possess.'

Only when I boldly confess then and then only do I
possess.

Mark 4:26 (NKJ) *And He said, 'The kingdom of*
God is as if a man should scatter seed on the ground.'

Now as I said before, we can imagine the kingdom of God
with angels flying around in throne room; with thousands
and millions of saints around the throne worshipping the
Father who sits on the throne. But Jesus never gave us that
picture. He said the kingdom of God is as a man scattering
seed on the ground (**Mark 4:26**).

Mark 4 is all about sowing seed. God uses a farmer, scattering seed, to explain how the kingdom works. The whole
concept is that the heart is soil. The word of God is seed,
and you sow it with your mouth, it goes into your ear and
into your heart. So that's the theme, that's the concept. This
is what our Lord is establishing in **Mark 4**. The kingdom of
God is you and me scattering seed in the ground, which
refers to us speaking what God says into our heart. That's
how the kingdom of God works; that's how it flourishes;
that's how it extends; that's how it progresses in this world.

Say this, 'I must speak the vision, the destiny, the purpose. I
must speak to the need.'

Humility is not keeping quiet. Humility is obedience to
God.

> **Mark 4:27 (NKJ)** ...*and should sleep by night and rise by day, and the seed should sprout and grow, he himself does not know how.*

Don't struggle, don't stress. God's seed does the work.

Say this, *"In the seed is the power to get the job done.* **Every seed has within itself the ability to produce its own harvest**. *So I have to speak the word and let the seed get the results for me."*

Humility is not keeping quiet. Humility is
obedience to God.

There are two ways we can achieve things in this world. **One**, by struggling in our own strength. **Two**, by speaking the word of God, planting the seed with your mouth, going to sleep, rising by day and allowing the seed to do its work. And what happens? We fight the good fight of faith by making sure we keep the seed in our heart. Then when faith comes, rest comes.

> **Hebrews 4:3 (NKJ)** *for we who have believed do enter that rest.*

That's a sign of faith in action. Resting and letting the seed do its job.

> **Romans 4:17 (NIV)** *As it is written: "I* **have** *made you a father of many nations." He is our father in the sight of God, in whom he believed—the God who gives life to the dead and calls things that are not as though they were.*

So here we see God said, *"I* **have** *made you."* Not 'I'm going to', but 'I have'. *"I* **have** *made you the father of many nations."* This was said **before** Isaac was born. Therefore God calls those things that be not as though they were.

Say this, *"If God says I have it before He sees it, it is okay for me to say I have it before I see it."*

> [18] *Against all hope, Abraham in hope believed and so became the father of many nations, just as it had been said to him, 'So shall your offspring be.'*
> [19] *Without weakening in his faith he faced the fact that his body was as good as dead.*

Abraham was 99 and Sarah his wife was slightly younger. He faced the reality that his body was as good as dead. Abraham could not have children any more. But he didn't let that stop him from saying what God said. God can change things and bring death to life if necessary. Without weakening his faith, he faced the fact that his body was as good as dead, since he was about 100 years old, and that Sarah's womb was dead. Thus you can say, 'By Jesus stripes I was healed,' even when your body's screaming with pain.

*[20] Yet he did not waver through unbelief regarding the promise of God, but was strengthened in his faith and **gave glory to God**.*

He did not waver but was strengthened in his faith. He did not waver through unbelief regarding the promise of God. What was the promise of God? "**You are the father of many nations**." His name was **Abraham, which means 'father of many nations'**. So he didn't waver at this promise, *"You are the father of many nations."* But, it says, he was strengthened in his faith and **gave glory to God**. I prefer that statement in the New King James, which reads, *"...was strengthened in faith, giving glory to God."* In other words his faith was strengthened by **giving glory to God**.

Say that, "**Abraham's faith was strengthened by giving glory to God**." Or say it this way, *"By praising God our faith is made stronger."*

My faith works better when I say my confession of faith in a praise format. For example, *"Praise God, by Jesus' stripes I am healed."* **Then act healed**.

Philippians 4:6 (NKJ) *Be anxious for nothing...*

Don't worry, and don't get stressed out.

...but in everything by prayer and supplication...

That means heartfelt prayer.

> ...with **thanksgiving** *let your request be made*
> *known to God.*

Say this, *"I must make my prayer request and include thanks-giving."* I must praise God when I ask for something, or when I use my faith. I need to turn my confession into a praise format because that's the instruction.

> **Colossians 2:7 (NKJ)** ... *Established in the faith*
> *as you have been taught, abounding in it with*
> *thanksgiving.*

Say, *"My faith abounds when I include thanksgiving in my confession."* My faith abounds. It goes over the top when I include thanksgiving in my confession. The best release of our faith is when we combine praise in our confession. That's exactly what Abraham did here. He was strengthened in his faith by giving glory to God.

How would we do that today? We could say, *"Praise God by Jesus' stripes I was healed."* Or we could say, *"I thank you Jesus for healing me with your stripes. Thank you Jesus for healing me by your stripes."* Or we could say, *"Thank you Jesus for meeting all my needs according to your riches in glory by Christ Jesus."* Or, *"Thank you Father for meeting all my needs according to your riches in glory by Christ Jesus."* We can thank God in our confession as we make it, and that's what Abraham did. Abraham said, *"Praise God I am the father of many nations,"* because that's what his name is. *"Praise God I am the father of many nations."* Or he might have said, *"Father God, thank you for making me the father of many nations."* Abraham was strengthened in faith, giving glory to God as he made his confession, *"I am the father of many nations."*

We can see God calls those things that do not exist as though they did. We could say that everything is fine when it's not fine. We say everything is great when the wheels are coming off.

Look at the Shunnamite woman whose son died. She put his body in the prophet Elisha's room. Then she traveled to a distant country to find Elisha. She didn't even tell her husband that their son was dead. Elisha saw her a great way off and he sent Gehazi, his servant, to her. He said, *"Go find out what the Shunnamite woman wants."* Gehazi asked, *"Is it well with you, is it well with your son?"* She said, *"It is well. Everything's fine."* She was not going to confess, *"My son's dead."* She was not willing to put his death in concrete.

We are not to talk about the bad finances, and the bad economy. We are not to say, *"My brother will never get saved. My father, or my mother will never get saved. They keep rejecting the gospel. Those folks at work are heathens they just don't want to know. They'll never want to know."* We're to say, *"Everything's fine. They love Jesus. They love God. They're going to serve God with all their hearts."* I know that sounds crazy, but God calls those things that are not as though they were, and if He can do it then we can do it. That's how faith works.

If I believed God for a pulpit, and I get one, I don't need faith anymore. I need faith to get it here. Faith has to be used before we see the thing. He calls things that He wants and things He desires as if He's got it now. That's how God does it.

> **Genesis 12:1 (NLT)** *The Lord had said to Abram, 'Leave your country, your relatives and your father's house, and go to the land I will show you.*
>
> [2] *'I will make you a great nation. I will bless you;*

What does that mean, *"I'll make you into a great nation"?* Abraham had no kids. That means he was going to have kids. Abraham could have said right there, *"Praise God, I'm going to have children. Praise God, He is giving me children."* He and Sarah would have had Isaac. He didn't say it. There's no record of Abraham ever adding his confession to God's word.

> **Genesis 12:4 (NKJ)** *So Abram departed as the Lord had spoken to him, and Lot went with him. And Abram was seventy-five years old when he departed from Haran.*

They went from Ur of the Chaldeans to Haran, and they waited there for five years before they went on to Canaan. Abram was seventy-five years old when God told him, *"You're going to have children."*

> **Genesis 15:5 (NKJ)** *Then He (God) brought him (Abraham) outside and said, 'Look now toward heaven, and count the stars if you are able to number them.' And He (God) said to him, 'So shall your descendants be.'*

God said, *"count the stars if you can."* There are trillions of stars, scientists have been able to measure stars up to 250 million light years away. Think of all the stars out there.

> *[6] And he (Abraham) believed in the Lord, and He (God) accounted it (Abraham's faith) to him (Abraham) for righteousness.*

We see in verse 6 that Abraham said **in his heart**, *"I agree."* **He didn't say it with his mouth** but he believed in his heart. Now, let's skip down to:

> **Genesis 17:1 (NKJ)** *When Abram was ninety-nine years old...*

That's 24 years later.

> *...the Lord appeared to Abram and said to him, 'I am the mighty God. Walk before me and be blameless.'*
>
> *[5] 'No longer shall your name be called Abram, but your name shall be called Abraham for I have made you a father of many nations.'*

"Your name is going to be called 'father of many nations' because that's what I have made you." **I have** made you, not going to. Isaac was not born yet, but He said, *"I* **have** *made you."* Now whenever Abraham introduced himself he said, *"I am father of many nations"*, (because that was his new name). Why did God change his name? In order to force him to confess the promise. Abraham believed it for 24 years but didn't say it, so nothing happened. Therefore God made him say, *"I am the father of many nations,"* by making his name, *"father of many nations."* At ninety-nine years of age he started to say, *"I am 'father of many nations,'"* and a year later, Isaac is born.

> **Genesis 21:5 (NKJ)** *Now Abraham was one hundred years old when his son Isaac was born to him.*

It took three months for his faith to grow to maturity, for it to produce the harvest. His confession produced the harvest of his body working again, and his wife Sarah's body working again, and a seed to be planted in Sarah's womb.

> **Genesis 15:5 (NKJ)** *Then He (God) brought him (Abraham) outside and said, 'Look now toward heaven, and count the stars if you are able to number them.' And He said to him, 'So shall your descendants be.'*
> *⁶ And he believed in the Lord…*

God had to make Abraham say it because he believed but he didn't say it. Jesus said in:

> **Mark 11:23 (NKJ)** *For assuredly, I say to you, whoever **says** to this mountain, 'Be removed and be cast into the sea,' and does not doubt in his heart, but believes that those things he **says** will be done, he will have whatever he **says**.*

He has what he says if he believes in his heart what he says with his mouth. Abraham believed in his heart, but he didn't say it with his mouth. We have to **say and believe** for it to work. Remember what we learnt in:

> **Luke 17:6 (NKJ)** *So the Lord said, 'If you have faith as a mustard seed, **you can say** to this mulberry tree, 'Be pulled up by the roots and be planted in the sea,' and **it would obey you**.*

Say this, *"Faith works like a seed, and my faith comes out of the seed."*

God's word is seed and we hear the word and it brings faith. When we have the seed, when we have the word; we have the faith. This is your destiny. Whether it's a written promise from God's word, or a spoken promise from the Holy Spirit to your heart — if you have that seed in your heart, you have the faith to say it, because faith comes out of the seed. Jesus said, *"if you have faith as a seed you can say."* You can't say and expect a result if you don't have the seed in your heart. The faith to say comes out of the seed. But if you have the word in your heart you **must** say, otherwise it's not going to happen.

God gave Abraham the promise (the seed) and all Abraham had to do was plant the seed. But he did **not** plant the seed, so Isaac was not born. God gave Isaac to Abraham in a seed when Abraham was 75 years old. In essence, God said to Abraham, *"Here is the seed for Isaac to be born. You will have as many children as there are stars in the sky."* And again the second time, *"You will have children if you will go to the Promised Land"* (as seen in **Genesis 12**). That was Isaac in a seed, but Abraham never confessed it, therefore God changed his name so that he would confess it.

Say this, *"God wanted Jesus to come to the earth through Isaac. Even so, God couldn't force Abraham to have Isaac. God had to get Abraham to use his faith first, before He could do it through Abraham and Sarah."*

That means no matter how desperate God is for us to have what we need, and what we want, He can't help us until we say what we believe, until we say the promise, until we speak out the destiny God has given us. **We are not to speak about the problem but speak of the solution**. The solution will change the problem.

Say this, *"Christians will never have what they say until they stop saying what they have."*

> We are not to speak about the problem but speak
> of the solution.

God will never take control of our lives against our will. He will never force us into His blessings, regardless of how desperate He is for us to have them, until we say what the blessing is and that it is ours. We must pull up the weeds we have planted in our heart through the years. Let's pull them out because if we don't, they will choke the word that we try and put into it. We've programmed our heart to think certain things about ourselves, about our limitations, and about our character. Some people have allowed what others have done to them to affect their actions and their beliefs about themselves. Some people have a poor self-image because they've allowed negative things that have happened to them, or been spoken about them, to go into their heart.

There are wonderful people who can be in a conversation with someone and they will start thinking, 'These people are talking about me. Oh, they are saying this about me, or they don't like this about me.' The others are not talking about them, but they start imagining that they are. If you try and help them they just get upset, they put their porcupine quills out. *"Don't come near me with that. I want to hang onto my problems. Don't try and fix me."* They are hurting so much you can't help them. It is all weeds in their heart.

133

Remember, when you see someone in church, you only see their good behavior. You see their Colgate smile. You only see their good side. You don't see them at home when they're messing up. But you see yourself when you're messing up and you compare yourself to someone else when they're perfect, in church, with a Bible in their hand. We are all absolutely nothing without Jesus. All we have is from God. We should see ourselves as God sees us. Not as we see ourselves in the natural with our natural limitations. God made us in Christ as a new creation born of the second Adam. We are to see who we are in Christ with **His** righteousness, **His** wisdom, **His** strength, **His** ability, and **His** love. God loves you desperately, more than He loves His own life. He gave His life for you, that is how much He loves you. You are blessed and highly favored of God and Jesus Christ is in you and me. 'It's not I that liveth but Christ who is alive in me.' He thinks through us, He walks through us, He talks through us, He loves through us, His character is in us, and His nature is in us.

Stop looking at yourself in the natural and look at yourself as God says you are. Looking at ourselves in the natural causes strife, and competitiveness, it causes pathetic squabbles and jockeying for position, which are from the devil. It has nothing to do with God. There's nothing like that going on between the Father, the Son and the Holy Spirit. Can you imagine the Son saying, *"Now Father, you've been sitting on that throne long enough, it is my turn. When am I going to have a turn?"* There's no such thing. Let's see each other as God sees us, and stop comparing ourselves with each other's natural abilities. Let's uproot those bad emotions from our heart, our production center. Each one of us has unique talents, gifts and anointings from God, equipping us to do what God has called us to do. As soon as we start doing what we were designed to do by God, and begin using our faith, it will show.

Just like a duck when it swims on water, or an eagle when it flies, you will find when you start following God's plan for your life, and start operating with the gift God gave you, you will fulfill that plan. Start saying, **Colossians 1:9**, *"I am continually receiving the knowledge of God's will, for every area of my life, in all spiritual wisdom and understanding, that I might fully please the Father in all things."*

Say this, "In the name of Jesus I root out of my heart everything related to my old carnal nature — selfishness, greed etc. I forgive all those who have offended me. I am determined to only have good soil in my heart. From now on, my heart is free to receive the seed of the word of God. God's word will work in my life. I am rising to the top.

"In the name of Jesus I declare Christ is in me. He lives in me. Greater is He that is in me than every challenge I meet. He thinks through my mind. He speaks through my lips. He loves through me. His nature is seen in me. I'm blessed of God, I am highly favored. I am a blessing to everybody I speak to. People love me because I am a blessing from God. I love people. God sends people to bless me all the time. Praise God, I am flowing in the abundance of God's blessings."

Chapter Eight

Believing What We Speak

2 Corinthians 4:13 (NKJ) *And since we have the same spirit of faith, according to what is written, 'I believed and therefore I spoke,' we also believe and therefore speak,*

Paul was quoting from **Psalm 116:10** and said we have the same spirit of faith as the Old Testament saints. Then Paul added to that statement from the Old Testament with these words, "**we also believe and therefore speak**." What Paul is saying is, since we have the same spirit of faith as the Old Testament saints which causes them to believe and speak, we in the New Testament also believe and speak. Paul said, '**that the spirit of faith is one that believes and says what it believes.**' It's not just a believing and it's not just a speaking, but it's a **combination** of **believing** and **saying**. We understand that this applies primarily to sharing our faith with others, teaching others about Jesus and receiving Christ, witnessing for the Lord. But if that is how we are supposed to use our faith in helping others to receive Christ, then that is the same principle we ought to apply in believing God for anything else we need in this life. Not only are the souls of our family and friends to be saved, and lives to be changed, we are also to believe God for material things that we need. We are to believe what

God's word says, and then say what God's word says. We're not to **just** believe it, but we are to repeat it if we have the same spirit of faith, because the spirit of faith is that spirit which believes and says. The Bible calls faith a **spirit** and we know that faith ultimately comes from God. Therefore faith is God's Spirit in action. The Spirit of God brings faith to our hearts through the word.

The Bible said we have not been given a **spirit** of fear (**2 Timothy 1:7**). Therefore we know that fear is also a spirit, but it is a demon spirit. We must not allow ourselves to fear, this gives demons the opportunity to work against us. We must believe and speak what God says. This allows God's Spirit to work. Faith is the cure, the antidote for fear, and it comes from God's word.

> **Hebrews 10:23 (NKJ)** *Let us hold fast the confession of our hope without wavering, for He who promised is faithful.*

The Lord who promised to do what He said, is faithful to do what He said. The Old King James says, 'Hold fast to your confession of faith without wavering.' Whether you are speaking out your hope or you're speaking out what you believe, either way, the moment you declare something to be so, whether it is the hope you declare or whether it is something in your heart you believe and you declare, the moment you declare it, it becomes an act of faith.

As long as your actions don't contradict what you say, Satan cannot stop God's word from working for you. When you say something that you believe God is going to do for you, don't change your confession the next day. To give you an example:

> **John 16:23 (NKJ)** ... *Whatever you ask the Father in My name, He will give you.*
> [24] ... *Ask and you will receive, that your joy may be full.*

The Lord said if we don't have full joy, we should ask for what we need, so that our joy can be full.

As long as your actions don't contradict what you say, Satan cannot stop God's word from working for you.

Let's imagine a precious lady who hasn't been married, sits in our service and hears the message that is in this book. She drives home and prays, *"Father, in the name of Jesus according to* **John 16:23**, *I ask you for a husband."* She describes her husband to God and says, *"This is what I'd like him to be and this is what I'd like him to look like."* Then she says, *"Now Father, Jesus said if I ask you for something using His name, that you would grant my request and you would provide it. I believe you have heard my prayer and I believe you* *are taking care of this. I praise you Father, I have a husband."* Would it be unscriptural for her to do that?

Let's imagine you needed $200 very urgently. It is 9 o'clock at night and you're sweating. Tomorrow morning, when you get to your office, you have to pay $200. So you phone John, a friend who you know is faithful and trustworthy, and you say, *"John, I have a real problem. I need to borrow $200 and I've got to have it tomorrow morning."* He says, *"Hey, don't worry about it. In the morning I'll drive over and I will give you $200."* You say, *"Thank you John,"* put the phone down and you go to your spouse and say, *"Honey, Praise God the problem is solved. John is bringing us the money tomorrow morning on the way to work. I'll have the money when I go to the office, praise God."* You go to sleep and you rest peacefully.

The Bible said, *"They that believe have entered into rest."* The minute you're in faith, you have peace in your heart. If there's any stress or unrest, you know you're not in faith yet. So stay with the scripture, meditate on it and say it to yourself until rest comes. Then you know you have entered faith. Now if we can believe the word of a trusted reliable friend to bring $200 over in the morning, and sleep peacefully, can we not have the same trust in God who said, *"Whatever you ask the Father, in my name, He will give you. Ask, and you will receive, that your joy may be full"*?

Let's go back to the woman who prayed for a husband. She has the same faith in God's promise as you have in John's promise on the phone for $200, so she goes home praising God. She gets into bed that night with her hands raised and praising God for her husband. She falls asleep, probably dreams about her husband, and the wedding day. She wakes up in the morning and she is alone. She feels sad. Maybe she has the Monday blues. She says, *"When will I ever have a husband? When is God ever going to give me a husband?"* What has she done? She's not holding fast to her confession of faith. She's ruined everything God had approved. God was in the process of bringing him, the angels had located him and they were bringing him to her. And the angels say, *"We have to stop, boys. Just when we had the whole Cupid deal wrapped up, we have to stop. Listen to this confession."*

Now family, there are twice as many angels as demons. The Bible said a third of the angels fell, and the devil is an angel who lost his anointing. God is still on the throne and Jesus is next to Him, the Holy Spirit is here. Stop worrying about the devil. The problem is this, there are too many people in our world saying negative things, and speaking bad things, and there are not enough people speaking good things. So there are more devils at work, because they are acting on all the bad things people say. There aren't enough angels at work because there aren't enough Christians speaking positive things. The angels are waiting for us to speak positively so they can get to work. Can you just see all the angels waiting? Drawn swords, powerful beings, waiting for the Christians to speak words of faith, so they can go into action. The angels say, *"I wish somebody would* give me something to do." And the devil says, *"I've got plenty to do with all the doubt, unbelief and sickness that's being spoken, the poverty that's being spoken, all the violence etc."* The demons are singing all the way to the bank.

Say this, *"I am going to speak positively, put the angels to work, and stop the demons."*

That dear lady should have woken up in faith the next morning and said, *"Praise God I have a husband."*

> **Hebrews 11:1 (NKJ)** ... *Faith is the evidence of things not seen.*

That's a scripture we know so well. God accepts our confession of faith as evidence that it is done. It is evidence in God's high court in heaven. For example, the lady says, *"Praise God I have a husband because Jesus said whatever you ask the Father in my name, He will give you. Ask, and you will receive, that your joy may be full. Praise God, based on* **John 16:23**, *I have a husband."*

God said that statement of her faith is **evidence** that she has a husband. God's high court says, *"There's the evidence, it's done."* When she gets married and she touches her husband, then touching her husband will be the evidence that she has one. But until she can touch him and see him and kiss him, her statement of faith is the evidence that she has a husband.

Say this, *"The word of God and my confession of it, is evidence in God's kingdom that I have it now. That's all the proof God needs, because He grants it and He takes care of it while I praise and confess it's mine. It is on its way with my name on it from the time I declared it is mine."*

You've got to see your name on it from the time you say it's yours. If you are confessing that you have a new job and you've got the description of your job written out, say, *"I **have** that job, God is guiding me to it."*
We could say, *"I am prospering,"* before we see the prosperity, or before we see the money.
We can say, *"I am well,"* before we see the healing in our bodies.
We can say, *"I live a holy life by the grace of God,"* even while the devil is tempting us, even when we are going through temptation.

If we don't say it, we are not going to win. The moment we say it, we begin to move into victory. We must say, *"Thank you Father for keeping my thoughts holy,"* while the devil is trying to put unwanted thoughts into our mind. It doesn't matter who we are, the greatest saint of God will find thoughts in their mind that they don't want to think from time to time. The devil is so tricky, he will put a thought into your mind and then he will tell you, *"You can't be a good Christian, otherwise you would never have thought that thought."* We have to discern where those thoughts are coming from. We know it's the devil because we wouldn't want to do those things. We catch ourselves saying, *"Where did that thought come from? I don't want to think like that."* Then we know it's the devil. There are a few things we can do about that. Firstly, don't get condemned; don't feel guilty and bad. It's not your thought. Tell the devil straight away, *"I know that's you, devil, and you can't bluff me."* You can just laugh it off if you wish, or simply tell the devil, *"I resist you Satan, in the name of Jesus,"* and ignore it because you haven't sinned.

The only time we sin with our thought life is if we accept that thought, start to meditate on it, fantasize about it, and then act on it. Get my message titled, '**Standing Against The Storm In Your Mind**' taught in Johannesburg in May 2013 to learn more about how to stand against those kinds of thoughts.

This is what Paul the Apostle said to the jailer who wanted to be saved, when God shook the jail and the chains fell off all the prisoners:

> **Acts 16:31 (NKJ)** *'Believe on the Lord Jesus Christ, and you will be saved, you and your household.'*

You can take that scripture and say, *"Praise God I believe my whole family is saved because if God made a promise to the jail keeper He surely means that we can claim it too."* Perhaps members of your family are living just like the devil, they're running with the wrong crowd, maybe some of them are in jail right now. But you can say, *"Praise God, I believe all my family are saved. Me and my household."* When we do that, the angels go to work, they begin working on those family members, and the demons get pushed aside. *"Get out of here demons, you heard what she said! We're working on this case now. Sorry boys, out you go."* But if we ever say stuff like, *"Oh you know my family, they are just a bad bunch of people. Most have ended up in jail and I guess the rest will too."* When you say stuff like that, the demons go to work and the angels say, *"I wish that she didn't say that."*

Maybe your kids are running wild, doing things they shouldn't be doing. Just raise your hands and praise God every day. *"Father I see them serving You with all their hearts, I see them free. Praise God, I and my household shall be saved, so I see them praising God and serving God in church."* That makes the angels work and makes the devil stop. If somebody in our family says something negative, we can help each other. We tell each other to say positive things and plant the good seed.

Let's look again at the single lady. She says, *"Oh well you know I've waited so long, I don't know if it's ever going to happen."*
Right there we can catch her and say, "Let's pull up that bad seed. Say this, 'I repent for saying that.'"
And she says, *"I repent for saying that."*
Then you say, "Now make a bold positive confession. 'Praise God I believe I have a husband.'"
We make her pull up the bad weed and plant the good seed. Don't just say, *"Don't say that anymore."* Pull it out right

there. Change the confession. You don't want weeds to grow in your heart.

Why does the Bible say in **Hebrews 10:23**, *"hold fast to your confession of faith"*? Here is a demonstration of holding fast. Let's say we choose eight men, four on each side of a rope. Those men are going to have a little tugging contest, and whoever pulls the other team past a line on the floor is the winning team. But let's say one team doesn't hold tight. They are just smiling and goofing around. When I say 'go', they are playing around. But the other team pulls. What happens to the rope? It comes out of their hands, because they weren't ready, they were not paying attention. God said, *"hold fast to your confession,"* because the devil is pull-ing on the other side. He's trying to pull it away from you. That is exactly what Jesus said in **Mark 4**. Jesus said the devil comes **immediately** to steal the word and he brings problems, circumstances, things to confuse us, things to distract us, so that we forget about making our confession.

I will hold fast my confession of faith without wavering because I know the devil is pulling on the other side.

Back to the single woman — she wakes up the next morn-ing and doesn't say, *"Praise God I have a husband."* She forgets to say it for three or four days, then she comes to church and hears the message, **The Power of Positive Words** and says, "Oh, I didn't say, 'I have a husband the whole week!'" At that rate it's going to take a while! She might end up like Sarah and get married at ninety years of age! We want to make sure we hold fast to our confession of faith, and not let the devil steal the word out of the heart or stop us from making our bold confession of faith.

Say this, *"I will hold fast my confession of faith without wavering because I know the devil is pulling on the other side."*

If we walk in faith, that doesn't mean that we will never have any challenges in our life, or that we are going to live on our Father's yacht forever. Not at all, the devil is going to try and discourage us, and he's going to try and attack us, he will try and steal the word. Since we've got the word now, the devil's paranoid, he's afraid of us. He's a lot more afraid of us than we are of him, that's why he comes immediately to steal the word. He knows you have a lot more word in you, so he's panicking. He doesn't know what to do about this. So if a problem comes our way, we have the victory, we know what to do. But we must not think problems will **never** come our way, just because we have an understanding of how to use the word of God and walk in faith.

> **Luke 6:47 (NKJ)** *Whoever comes to Me, and hears My sayings and does them, I will show you whom he is like:*

Right now we are looking at the sayings of Jesus.

> [48] *He is like a man building a house, who dug deep and laid the foundation on the rock. And when the flood arose, the stream beat vehemently against that house and could not shake it, for it was founded on the rock.'*

This is not only talking about building a natural house. It's talking about our life. The life that's built on the rock will not be shaken. I've asked people around the world, *"What is the rock that we should build on so that our life is not shaken?"* People tell me it is Jesus. That's wonderful, but that's not what Jesus said here. People tell me that it is praying a lot. That's wonderful too but that's not what Jesus said here. People say, *"Well Pastor Theo, building my life on the rock means that I will live a holy life."* Again, that's marvelous, but that's not what Jesus said here. No, He said that building our life on the rock is to **hear** the word and **act** on the word. Do it! Do what you hear.

> **Luke 6:47 (NKJ)** *Whoever comes to Me, and hears My sayings and **does** them, I will show you whom he **is** like:*

Say this, *"In order for me to have a life that's unshaken by storms of life, by circumstances; in order for me to have a life that the devil cannot move or destroy, cannot even shake, I simply have to hear the word and do the word."*

Some folks believe we go to church on Sunday to ease our conscience. They think, *"If I go to church, I'll be doing a won-*

derful deed, and all I have to do is show my face, warm my chair, and then I will be a great Christian and all is well. No storms of life will get me." I assure you now that's not the case. To be a **hearer** only and **not** a doer gets us into trouble. If we will do the word of God, it will work, strangely enough. There is more to living a victorious Christian life that can't be shaken then just presenting ourselves in church on a Sunday. God has principles that He gives us in His word, and if we apply them, we can live a life that cannot be destroyed by the devil.

> *49 But he who heard and did nothing is like a man who built a house on the earth without a foundation, against which the stream beat vehemently; and immediately it fell. And the ruin of that house was great.'*

He heard the word, but didn't act on it, so the house was ruined by the storm. You and I know good Christians who love God with all their hearts and yet the storms of life have destroyed them. We know other Christians who face the storms of life one after the other, but they're still standing, they're still witnessing, they're still leading souls to Christ, they still come to church, they're still smiling and we just wonder how on earth are they standing? How is it possible? But didn't Jesus tell us it is the same storm that comes to two different houses? The one house is totally destroyed and the other house stands; it's not even shaken.

Say this, "**It's not the storms of life that destroy us**. *It's what we* **say** *about them, and it's what we* **do** *about them."*

Next time somebody comes to you and says, *"Look at this serious problem. What on earth are we going to do?"* Tell them, *'***I know what we're going to do. We're going to just act like the Bible's true and do what the Bible said.***"* We will have a house that cannot be shaken when we do that. It's just that simple. Hold fast to your confession when you go through the storm.

> It's not the storms of life that destroy us.
> It's what we say about them, and it's what we do
> about them.

There are **three** things I'd like to mention about the storms of life. The devil is very subtle. He will tell you, *"This storm has come to you; this problem has come your way because you're not a good Christian. It's no good you praying about it because God is not going to answer your prayer. After all, you're a bad Christian."* Or the devil is going to say, *"You know you caused this problem. Do you remember so-and-so? You caused that problem, therefore don't pray to God about this, He's not going to help you out of this problem because it's your fault."* But let's analyze this to see if that's correct or not. **Firstly**, the main reason why 99.99% of all problems come our way is because Jesus said in **Mark 4, 'Satan comes immediately to steal the word.'** He comes to take away God's **word** so you forget it or don't apply it, because the

word is your ability to succeed. So he will bring all these confusions, these problems to distract you.

Remember God loves you more than words can ever explain. Here is a picture to try and explain how much God loves you. Look at Jesus on the cross; He was on there for you.

Like the single woman who started confessing, *"Praise God I have a husband,"* then suddenly calamities come her way on Monday morning. The following Sunday she realizes she hasn't made her confession for a husband, because she has been so distracted by all the problems the devil caused.

The **second** reason problems come, is because sometimes we make decisions without praying about them. I'm not talking about normal decisions, going to work, coming home, going to church, doing the everyday things. If we make a mistake in any of those decisions we will not open the door to the devil. If I put on a red tie instead of a blue one, I will not open the door to the devil. It's the decisions we make that we should pray about. For example, going to live in another city. You never want to do that unless you spend time praying about it. You should be fully persuaded in your heart that God is guiding you to do that.

> ***Acts 17:26 (NIV)*** *From one man he made every nation of men, that they should inhabit the whole earth; and he (God) determined **the times set for them** and the **exact places** where they should live.*

> **Ecclesiastes 6:10 (NLT)** *Everything has already been decided. It was known long ago what each person would be.* **So there's no use arguing with God about your destiny.**

Everything will change if you make a decision to live in another city if God didn't tell you to. You need to have a knowing in your heart, and a peace in your heart. If you have unrest, if you are afraid about it, or you are unsettled in your spirit, don't do it. If you have a peace and joy, you know this is what God wants, then go for it. It will bring blessing. We are to pray about destiny-defining decisions we make in life. But we don't have to pray for half an hour to see if we should get out of bed in the morning. We don't have to spend another two hours praying to see which tie to put on. When we arrive at the office at 3 o'clock and say, *"Boss, I had to pray and see if God wanted me to work today or not."* He will say, *"I know the answer to that question, God doesn't want you to work here at all. Leave now."*

Let us continue with the **second** way problems may come. They may come if we do not pray and pay attention to the leading of the Holy Spirit. When there's danger ahead, the Holy Spirit will always warn you.

Say this, *"Danger will never come my way without the Holy Spirit endeavoring to warn me about it first."*

For example, if you are on your way to work, and the Holy Spirit says, *"Don't go that way, go this way,"* listen to that guidance. If the Holy Spirit says, *"Don't marry this person."*

Listen to that guidance. This is especially true if they are not saved because your father is God and their father is the devil. If you get married to someone like that you're going to have a lot of trouble with your father-in-law because the devil will then be your father-in-law. We have to listen to the Holy Spirit as He guides us. We don't want to make wrong decisions. Now if you make a wrong decision by not listening when there is danger ahead and you go into it, you will go into the storm.

For example, in 1997, we, the church, set out to build a huge complex on our 33 acres of land. An offer was made that seemed wonderful, I got so excited about it, I accepted it without praying, and without listening for God's guidance. The end result of that was it wasn't God, it wasn't a God-given opportunity, and we had to eventually tear that building down. We got into millions of dollars worth of debt. It took us three years to pay that debt off. For a period of six months it looked like the ship was going to sink every day. We did not know if we would make it one day past another in the natural. I went away for a few days, to seek God about the matter. The Lord said, *"I will not do one big miracle for you, and deliver you like I did in 1985, this is going to be a series of little miracles, little answers to prayer over a period of months, but you are going to have to go through the storm, because you didn't listen. I would have prevented you going into the storm if you had listened."*

Paul was on the way to Rome to make an appeal to Caesar. He boarded a ship, which was supposed to dock for winter at Crete. Paul perceived in his heart that there was much danger ahead for them and the ship. He went to the Captain and the ship's owner and said, *"I perceive danger ahead and even the loss of our lives."* The captain and the owner said, *"No, we are going ahead,"* because the weather looked perfect. They set sail, but hit a huge storm that almost destroyed their lives. All hope was lost. The ship was destroyed but the Lord intervened. After some days of fasting and prayer, an angel of the Lord appeared to Paul and said, *"Fear not Paul, God's going to save you and all those traveling with you."* He went and told everybody on the boat, *"Not one hair on your head will be lost but this ship is going to be destroyed on an island."* The boat was wrecked on the island of Malta but they were all saved. Because the Captain and the owner of the ship did not listen to Paul, they went **through** the storm. If they had listened to Paul, they would have stayed in the harbor and **avoided** the storm altogether.

I went **through** the storm because I didn't listen to God initially. Now there have been many times when I heard the voice of God and a storm was **avoided**.

Pastor Bev almost died; she was almost murdered by four men. The spirit of God warned me, and I began to intercede and supernaturally her life was spared. Several years ago a huge steel gate, weighing many pounds fell on Candace, but the spirit of God had warned me about it beforehand, I began to intercede, and when it happened, Candace wasn't hurt. In fact, she wasn't even bruised. Natalie could have been raped and murdered in the bush, but the Spirit of God warned me beforehand, and I interceded for her, and her life was spared. Even though the man had her down on the ground, he could do nothing to her.

Say this, *"Now I know, not every open door is from God. I have to listen to God's voice. If I have a peace, I do it. If I don't — if I have unrest — I don't do it."* **Listen to my message, 'The Mystery of the Open Door' taught in Johannesburg in October 2009 to learn more about how to recognize when God is guiding you**.

Ninety nine percent of our problems come our way because the devil's trying to steal the word. But if you start living a life of sin, and you don't repent, you know the devil has an opportunity of attacking you in many different ways. But if you say, *"God forgive me,"* from that moment on, you close the door on the devil. We all make little mistakes — that is not going to give the devil an opportunity to attack us. We are talking about deliberately living in a sin. We know we shouldn't be living this way, but we don't care. Most of us are doing our best to live right and the devil is trying to attack us because he wants to steal the word. He has no legal right to attack us, but he tries any way.

Say this, *"The devil has no legal right to attack me and I have not opened the door, therefore I hold fast to my confession of faith and the storms of life will not destroy me. In the name of Jesus, I and my house will not be shaken. In the name of Jesus, I understand I must hear the word, confess the word, and act like it is true no matter what comes my way. I am going through in*

154

victory because the word of God says, 'In all these things, right in the middle of these things, in the heat of the battle, 'Yet in all these things we are more than conquerors through Him who loved us,' according to **Romans 8:37**."

"As I hold fast to my confession of faith, my covenant partner is fighting this fight for me. He loves me. He is on my side. This battle is the Lord's. Thank you Jesus, my Savior."

The **third** reason problems come is because of our wrong words. Or because of neglecting to speak creative words when faced with a problem.

Chapter Nine

Standing On Our Confession of Faith

Let's look at King Nebuchadnezzar of Babylon who made a statue of himself. The statue was 90 feet high and 9 feet wide, made out of solid gold. He called all the subjects of his kingdom from every province to come and bow down before the statue and worship it. Shadrach, Meshach, and Abednego were Hebrew boys, and were Daniel's friends, brought as slaves from Jerusalem. Since they were on fire for God, they would not bow down to an idol and serve any other God. That upset King Nebuchadnezzar, who called Shadrach, Meshach, and Abednego to stand before him in front of thousands of people, and he said, *"You must bow before this golden statue and worship it, and if you do not, I will throw you into a burning fiery furnace."* Let's pick up the story from:

> **Daniel 3:16 (NKJ)** *Shadrach, Meshach, and Abednego answered and said to the king, 'O Nebuchadnezzar, we have no need to answer you in this matter.*

We're not going to discuss this business of you throwing us in the burning fiery furnace.

> [17] If that is the case, our God whom we serve is able to deliver us from the burning fiery furnace, and He will deliver us from your hand, O king.

That's a very positive statement of faith. There is no doubt in there. They didn't say, "**Perhaps** our God will deliver us." They didn't say, "**Maybe** our God will deliver us. I hope our God's watching because if He is I'm sure He'll deliver us."

> [18] But **if not**, let it be known to you, O king, that we do not serve your gods, nor will we worship the gold image which you have set up.'

This verse has been the subject of many sermons, where the pastor has preached things like, "If God does not deliver us we still won't bow down and worship this golden image." Essentially, "if you don't throw us in, we're not going to worship this image, but if you do throw us in, **we won't either**." Let's look at this logically.

> [17] if you throw us in the fiery furnace God will deliver us.

The question is in verse 18.

> [18] But **if not**, let it be known to you, O king, that we do not serve your gods, nor will we worship the gold image which you have set up.'

I personally believe he's saying, "If you throw us in, God's going to deliver us, and **if you don't throw us in**, we're not going to serve your god and worship him." There are two points I'd like to make to help us understand that this 'if

not' didn't mean, *"if God doesn't save us, we won't worship your golden image."*

Firstly — it would have been a change in their confession. One minute saying, *"God will deliver us,"* and the next, *"and if He doesn't save us."* That would neutralize the first statement of faith. Therefore, God would not have delivered them, and we know God delivered them. They would have surely died if that were their confession. And they didn't die, so that couldn't have been their confession.

Secondly — if God doesn't deliver them and they get thrown into the fire they would die. To say, *"If you kill us we are not going to worship your image,"* doesn't make sense. That's like saying to a person with a gun, *"If you shoot me dead, I won't be your friend anymore. I'll never come visit you anymore. I promise you, if you kill me now. I will never help you again."* That doesn't make sense. So it's obvious they never made a statement of doubt.

Imagine, for example if the following discussion had taken place, they would have been in trouble. *"Hey Shadrach, you know what? We made that confession to the king and all these people heard us. Our God's going to deliver us, but if He doesn't deliver us before we get in that fire we are toast. We're just going to believe that this confession of yours works."* And Shadrach replied, *"Yeah, I'm believing God's going to deliver us before we get thrown into the fire."*

That's like saying, *"I believe I have the money, which I need by the end of the month. I believe it is coming before the end of the month, because if it doesn't come before the end of the month, I don't know what I'm going to do. I have to have it before the end of the month, if it doesn't come by then I'm in real trouble. But, in the name of Jesus I believe I have it now."* Can you see the mistake here? Putting deadlines on God gets us into all sorts of trouble — there is no faith in confessions like those. Sometimes we will go past our deadlines. However, we must believe we receive it the moment we pray.

Remember your future is God's past. He sees it altogether. He's omnipresent. God is living 2000 years in the future and He's living 2000 years in the past. God sees everything. There's no time with God. Time is an earthly thing. So, don't put restraints on God. You can go past the end of the month, and God will keep you. If you end up in the fiery furnace, God will keep you without the smell of smoke on your clothes.

Our confession should be, *"I **am** delivered, I **am** well, I **have** the money, my family **is** serving God, we **are** together, and this problem **is** resolved."* While the battle is raging, we say, *"We believe this matter is resolved. This battle is the Lord's and the victory is mine."* Our God is bigger than deadlines, so hold fast to your confession of faith, believe **you have got it now**, don't be concerned about your deadline.

> **Daniel 3:25 (NKJ)** *'Look!' he answered, 'I see four men loose, walking in the midst of the fire; and they are not hurt, and the form of the fourth is like the Son of God.'*

If you've never heard Oral Roberts' sermon, '**The Fourth Man**' I encourage you to get it, it's a great message. The king called them out, and then he made this incredible statement — remember this is the same king who only wanted people to worship his statue.

> **Daniel 3:29 (NKJ)** *Therefore I make a decree that any people, nation, or language which speaks anything amiss against the God of Shadrach, Meshach, and Abed-Nego shall be cut in pieces, and their houses shall be made an ash heap; because there is no other God who can deliver like this.'*

"If you say anything bad about their God, I'll cut you into little pieces." And he had the power to do it. *"And your houses shall be made an ash heap."* Or, I'll burn your house down, *"because there is no other God who can deliver like this."* Here was a heathen king who saw a miracle and became a God worshipper in a moment. He won his entire kingdom to the Lord. He got them all saved. He was a great soul winner; he had great techniques that we haven't thought about using in our modern world. He had persuasive ways of getting people to become believers in the God of Shadrach, Meshach, and Abednego, which I haven't heard in soul winning courses lately. Only kidding.

Say this, *"My God is the God of Shadrach, Meshach, and Abednego, and nobody can deliver me like my God can."*

They made their confession and they held fast to it. Going into the burning fiery furnace was pretty bad, don't you think? Especially if it was heated seven times hotter than usual. This is not a storybook, this really happened.

I'd like to share a true story of something that happened in my life to help illustrate that truth.

Going Past Deadlines

In 2008 I was flying into Johannesburg to minister there. We were probably about 10,000 feet up, approaching the outskirts of the city. As I looked out the window, I thought about something that I'd like to do, a desire that I had, and how much money I would need to do it. I decided to pray and ask the Father for this money. I used this scripture when I prayed:

> **Mark 11:24 (KJ)** *Therefore I say unto you, what things soever ye **desire** when ye pray, believe that ye receive them and ye shall have them.'*

It doesn't say, *"Whatever great need you have."* It doesn't say, *"Whatever life and death situation you have."* All that is correct, and if that is your situation that scripture would work for you. But I want to point out this is referring to a **desire** that you might have, not necessarily even a pressing need.

Whatever things you desire. **When** you pray, you have **to do something at the time of prayer**. **When** means time, look at your watch. When you pray, believe that you receive

them (them refers to the things you ask for) and you **shall** have them, future tense. **But you have to believe you have it when you pray**. That's what qualifies you to, 'shall have them.'

I asked the Father for money in this way. I said, *"Father, I ask you for this amount of money in the name of Jesus, for this purpose. And I ask that somebody will bring it to me while I'm here in Johannesburg this week.* **I believe I receive this prayer answered**. *I thank you for hearing my prayer. I believe it's my money* **right now**. *Someone in Johannesburg has got it, but it belongs to me. It's mine and while I'm here they will bring it to me. I* **have** *received it, it's done. I* **have** *the money."* It's as if you have the money right now in your bank account. You can't show it to me. But you have it, you own it, it's in your bank account. Does that make sense? I didn't pray, *"I'm going to get it, please Father won't you give it to me in the future?"* No, you have to pray and ask God for it now. If you're going to pray, believe and receive. That's the way to do it. I was using **Mark 11:24** here. So I am praying, believing I receive. If you pray it you still have to say it. When I saw Pastor Peter Cox that day I said, *"Hi, Pastor Peter. I just want you to know I have prayed and asked God for X amount of money and I received it, it is mine, and somebody is going to give me this money while I'm here."*

I could see by his face that he was choking on that, trying to swallow it, so I said to him, *"Look, don't think about it. Just say, 'I agree.'"*
He said, *"I agree."*

I said, *"Thank you."*

I didn't tell anybody else. There are some people you can't say anything to because it will just blow them away. There are times when you have to choose whom to tell, and there are times when you tell everybody. There are also times when you can only tell a select few. I wanted somebody I could confess it to. That's why I chose him, because I knew he would accept my confession. I was not saying it for his benefit. I was saying it for mine. A few days later I said it again. I said it to him a few times while I was there.

At the end of that week, I got back on that plane and we were flying out of Johannesburg when I remembered. Immediately the devil said to me, *"You didn't get it."* I reached down and got my little travel Bible, and opened it up to **Mark 11:24** and I read this verse out to the devil. I said, *"Mr. Devil, look at what Jesus said. 'Therefore I say unto you what things soever ye desire,* **when ye pray believe ye receive them**.*' I prayed. I received them when I prayed.* **I did that**. *Now look at what Jesus said, He said,* **'you shall have them**.*' It's mine. I own it.* **I have it because I did what Jesus said**. **Mark 11:24** *is my bank deposit slip. That's my guarantee.* **The word of God is the evidence**. *My faith in the word is the evidence of things you can't see."* I closed my Bible and I began to thank God. *"Father I thank you I* **have** *the money. Thank you for giving it to me."*

A few days went by and I got a phone call from Pastor Peter Cox. He said that somebody in the church called him, and told him he had this amount of money to give **me**. It was the exact amount that I asked for. They wanted to bring it to Pastor Peter after work that night, and they asked if he would he please stay late so they could give it to him. He said he would stay and wait at the office. The brother proceeded to tell Pastor Peter that while Pastor Theo was in Johannesburg the Lord told him to give Pastor Theo the money a few times, and he told his wife about it, but unfortunately things got in the way. He was distracted and time slipped away from him. He didn't get around to it. A few days after I had gone, the devil came to him and said, *"If you give that money to Pastor Theo, I will kill you and your family."* Pastor Peter told me that this man said, *"Pastor Peter I am really concerned. I've got to get this money out of my hands as soon as possible."*

Pastor Peter replied, *"Well, I'll be here."* That night he waited until late, but the man didn't come.

The next day, the man called again and apologized for not coming. Eventually he brought the money to Pastor Peter. Pastor Peter phoned me and said, *"I have the money, and this brother needs to talk to you and tell you why he didn't come as arranged. It is a very interesting story."* I said, *"Fine."* When I arrived back in Johannesburg on my next trip, I asked the brother to come to my office to pray with him, because when somebody gives you something you should always pray, *"Father in the name of Jesus, I am not the Lord of the harvest. I can't cause this seed to be multiplied back to this person, but you can. So I ask you to multiply it back to him and his family a hundred fold in the name of Jesus."* You pray and ask the Father for whatever the person is trusting God for, then you ask the Father to bless them and their family and their business etc. **Secondly**, I wanted to hear the story of why he didn't come. He proceeded to tell me that something had come up on the night he wanted to deliver the money, and his boss told him he had to work. So he asked his wife to deliver the money. She left with her children in the car. She put this cash into her purse (handbag) and put it into the trunk (boot) and locked it. They were driving to church, and were about five minutes away, on a three-lane freeway, doing 100 kilometers (65 miles) an hour in the slow lane. She happened to look up at the rear view mirror and saw a car behind her approaching at a very high speed with its lights flashing. She had nowhere to go. This car did not slow down but it ran straight into the back of her. She took off like a rocket off the freeway, lost total control of her car and crashed into the bush. The car behind her also went straight off the freeway into the bush. When she came to her senses, the first thing she did was check her family out and make sure they were all fine. She told her teenage son, *"Quickly check the trunk (boot) and bring me the purse with the money in it."* He got out and went to the back of the car, and saw that the back of the car was gone! The trunk (boot) was missing, and the whole back of the car was open like a burst coke can. He looked around for the purse. Finally he saw it lying by itself back where the impact took place, on the slow lane of the freeway. Cars obviously had slowed down because there was an accident. Everybody could see this purse. He ran back, picked up the purse, ran all the way to the car, got in and gave it to his mother. She checked the money and it was all there. As the man told me this story, the Lord spoke to me. I did not hear a voice at this time. There were no words, it came by revelation. Instantly the complete understanding of what happened in the spirit world dropped into my heart. Satan had said he was going to stop this family giving me that money at any cost. That was Satan's plan. He caused the accident. He took the purse out of the trunk. He put it on the freeway so it would be stolen. All these people were driving past, and some people were getting out of their cars. I had the revelation of the demons telling people, *"Hey, take that purse."* But in the spirit I could also see angels standing around the purse with drawn swords saying, *"You dare not touch that purse (handbag)."* The Lord said that if I had added one more thing to my confession, I would have gotten the money when I was in South Africa on my first trip. If I had said something like this, *"Satan, I bind you in Jesus' name, you will not interfere with the angels as they bring this money to me."* Then periodically said, *"I want to remind you devil, you are bound, you cannot touch that money, it's mine. It belongs to me"* (**Matthew 18:18**) (**James 4:7**). If I had done that I wouldn't have needed to wait until my second trip to receive the money. The devil would not have been able to do any of that. However, if I had done that I would not have had this lesson to share with you. For some reason it slipped my mind. But it re-emphasized the importance of saying, *"Devil, you are bound over my finances"*, or over whatever it is you are believing God for. We don't keep binding the devil. That's unbelief. We bind him once and then remind him that he is bound.

Say this, *"The devil will always try and hinder whatever we're believing God for. We must be aware of that."*

There is something else I would like you to see in regard to deadlines. I went past the deadline, I said I'd get the money when I was in Johannesburg, but I didn't. Flying out of Johannesburg I could have said, *"God did not answer my prayer."* I could have said, *"What went wrong?"* If I had said anything like that I would never have got that money. I held fast to my confession of faith flying out of Johannesburg, when I said, *"Praise God* **I have it now**. *It's mine."*

Say this, *"I must never give up. I must hold fast to my confession of faith. God is bigger than my circumstances."*

In 1979 Pastor Bev and I left Durban and moved to Johannesburg to start a church. We had saved enough money to build a home. We sensed the Holy Spirit tell us to give that money to start the new church with, so we opened a church bank account and deposited it into the account. The church began September 12th 1979. The Holy Spirit led us to go full time and trust God to supply our personal needs. We did. About two years later Harold Walton and Ian Peters led a motivation for the congregation to receive an offering for Pastor Bev and me to build a home. Six months later we gave that money to the church.

In 1983 Pastor Bev and I were renting accommodation, when we had a desire to look at houses on the market. We did not want to mislead any real estate agent, so we told them we wanted to look, but we had no money to buy anything. One realtor was willing to take us out every Monday afternoon. After a number of weeks we saw a home we really liked, 4 Barbara Road, Bedfordview. It was on one acre, with a pool and tennis court. When we got home, I went aside alone to pray. I sensed the Holy Spirit telling me to trust God for this house. I told Pastor Bev and she said, *"Let's pray."* I got a card and I wrote down four scriptures on one side, **Mark 11:23-24**, **John 16:23-24**. On the other side of the card I wrote the prayer: *"Dear Father in Heaven, we ask you for the R50,000 ($60,000) that we need as a deposit that we need to buy this house, in Jesus' name. We thank you for hearing our prayer and giving us this money. We praise and thank you for it in Jesus' name."* We meditated on the scriptures for about seven minutes. We prayed, then raised our hands and worshipped the Lord on our knees, next to the bed where we had prayed. We got up, and I phoned the realtor and told her that we wanted to sign an offer to purchase this home. She said, *"I thought you don't have any money?"* I never expected her to say that. I had to think fast. I said, *"Yes, you're right. That is what we said. I asked my father for the money and he said he would give me the R50,000 ($60,000)."*

She said, *"Is your father rich?"*

I said, *"Yes, very rich."*

She said, *"Well, tell him you have to pay the R50,000 in 30 days."*

I replied, *"That is not a problem. Let's sign the offer to purchase right now."* We did, and it was accepted.

No one knew about this, only Pastor Bev, the realtor and me. Within 30 days we received three checks, from three totally different people. Each one wrote a note and slipped it into the envelope with their check. 'This money is for you to buy a home'. The total of the three checks came to exactly R55,000. We paid the deposit of R50,000 and tithed the R5,000. Three years later we sold that house for a huge profit and gave all the money to the church. God helped us buy another home with no deposit required.

We have seen God do marvelous things in prayer. That is **The power of positive words**.

In 1984 I came home one day after work. I put my car in the garage, and walked towards the front door of our home. As I came past our swimming pool, I saw our full time gardener, Noel, with a long aluminum pole. At the end of it was a net and he was fishing berries out of our swimming pool. He was forever doing that because there was a berry tree in our neighbor's yard that hung over our six-foot high wall and our pool. So I said to the berry tree, *"You are plucked up by the roots."* In that same yard was another tree hanging over my tennis court. It was a huge tree — it must have been a hundred feet high. It had little acorns on it, little wooden things that looked like ice cream cones.

We couldn't play tennis because there were thousands of them all over the tennis court. So I said, *"and you also are plucked up by the roots."* For about six months, every time I saw those trees, I'd say, *"you are plucked up by the roots, you two trees."* I just said it. I didn't pray, I did not ask God to pick them up. I just used **Mark 11:23**.

One day I was standing at the pool having a discussion with Noel as he worked on the pool again. He had his aluminum pole with the net removing all the berries. I couldn't help feeling sorry for Noel. Just then our neighbor put her head over the wall and said, *"I'm so embarrassed about these berries in your pool."*

I asked, *"Would you mind if I trimmed back the branches here on my side of the fence, so that your tree doesn't drop its berries?"*

She said, *"Please go ahead."*

"Noel," I said, *"You heard the lady. Can you do that tomorrow?"* He said, *"No problem."*

After work the following day I came back to look at the trimmed branches, only to find the entire tree which was about 30 feet tall, gone. I looked over the wall and there was a two-foot high stump on the other side. I thought, *"Oh no, I had better go and see my neighbor."* I knocked on her front door, and when she came to the door, I said, *"Hi, did you notice we cut your tree back?"*

She said, *"Yes I noticed."* She was very observant!

I said, *"I am very sorry about that. That's not what I asked to be done but it happened and I take responsibility for it."*

She said, *"Oh, no, no, no. Don't apologize."* Then she said something that got my attention. *"You know, strangely enough, for the last six months that tree has been irritating me."*

Isn't that something? For the last six months I had been saying that tree was plucked up by the roots and it had been irritating her the whole time. She didn't act on the irritation, otherwise the tree would have been gone. Then I thought, *"Well, I've been confessing over that huge tree hanging over the tennis court as well. It is dropping all those little acorns all over my tennis court. I wonder if she is irritated about that tree as well?"*

I asked, *"How do you feel about that big tree at the other end of your property?"*

She said, *"That tree irritates me too."*

"Would you like us to take it out?" I asked.

She said, *"Would you?"*

I said, *"Sure we will."*

"Okay," she said, *"Go ahead."*

I spoke to Noel and told him that the neighbor wanted the other tree down and asked whether he could do it the next day. He said he could. I told him to get some of his friends to help him because it was such a large tree, but that I would pay them well for the day's work. He assured me he knew what he was doing. I finished up by saying, *"Noel, look, this tree has a fork right at the top of the tree, a huge big fork up there. Put a long rope through the fork and tie it around a small branch on the other side of the fork. Then, cut the branch off, and lower the branch down to the ground.*

Untie the rope, and repeat the procedure until you have cut all the branches off the top of the tree. Small pieces, little by little, cut the tree down."

Noel replied, *"This is not a problem, we can do this."*

The next evening I got a phone call from Pastor Bev while I was working at the office. *"You must come home now!"* She was freaking out, I mean, she was frantic. I could hardly make out what she was saying she was talking so fast. I managed to calm her down only to find out that this tree had fallen on the neighbor's house. A huge branch, it must have been 20 inches in diameter, had gone right across the entire house. I drove over immediately. The roof had caved in on the bed. The branch was lying on the walls at each end of this brick house with its tiled roof. All the tiles were now in the bedroom, on the bed. I knocked on her door. This time I didn't ask her if she'd noticed we'd cut her tree down. I had enough wisdom to not fool around with this one! The first thing I uttered was, *"I'm very sorry. We will fix the whole thing at our own cost. We'll do it immediately."*

She said, *"Thank you."* She wasn't a happy camper but she accepted that.

Anyhow, I went straight home and phoned Ben who owns a construction company. I told him I needed his help. I said, *"Please come out here right now."* When he arrived, I showed him the damage and told him that regardless of cost I needed him to fix it. *"I'll pay for it all, every cent,"* I told him.

He said, *"Pastor Theo, I'll tell you what. We'll take care of it just like you asked but you won't pay one cent, our company will take care of this."* He insisted on doing it for nothing. He would not take no for an answer. So I eventually thanked him and prayed for him. I had to find out what happened to Noel. The next day I asked him, *"Noel, tell me, what was your strategy here? What was your plan?"*

He said, *"We tied the rope over this big branch. All seven of my friends held the rope and I was at the end. I tied the rope around my waist in case they let go. I would be the anchorman. I would hold the branch."*

I thought, *"You are going to hold a branch weighing several tons?"*

As they went up into the air, these guys let go one at a time and fell to the earth. Fortunately they did not go too high before they let go, otherwise they could have died. Noel went up all the way until he got to the fork. Thank God the rope was long enough so he did not go through the fork, because that would have killed him. Anyway, somehow he got down and went home. But I thought about all this. *"I made the confession that these trees be plucked up by the roots. Something doesn't make sense. How come they were plucked up by the roots, but this disaster happened? I mean that wasn't part of the confession."*

I came to realize this one thing. When you make a confession of faith, you need to complete your confession, so that you don't give the **devil** a chance to get involved at the end of it. Be more specific with your confession. The same thing happened with the car crash, after praying for the money I needed (**Ephesians 4:27 (NKJ) ...nor give place to the devil**).

Jesus said to the mulberry tree, *"Be plucked up by the roots,"* he didn't leave it there, so it would fall on somebody's house. He said, **"and be cast into the sea**." He said, *"If any man says to this mountain be plucked up and* **cast** — *not onto somebody's house* — *but into the* **sea**." **He told the mountain where to go.**

I believe what we need to do is **be specific with our confession**.

Chapter Ten

Praying The Prayer Of Faith

Many people have this idea that pastors have a special prayer arrangement with God, a hotline that only they can use — straight into the throne room. No, we all go in the same way. I purposely want to share this next testimony with you, because it is something that happened long before I went into the full time ministry.

In 1975, at the end of October, I was standing in Beares showroom. They had at least 200, maybe 250 stores around South Africa, and were a very successful furniture retail business. They owned a number of high-rise buildings in West Street, Durban, the city in which I was born, grew up and was living at the time. They also owned buildings and shops in many other cities. I worked at their main branch in Durban and they had 17 salesmen in that store.

It was a Saturday morning and the floor was packed with people coming in to look at different items for sale. The showroom floor was large, with glass windows running right along the street front. People walking on the pavement could look in at the furniture all the way down the road through the long glass window.

I was standing about 30 feet, 10 paces from the door, expecting someone to walk in so I may serve them. I saw a white Peugeot station wagon pull up right outside, with a surfboard on the roof. I immediately recognized the car. My friend, Sam Stark, jumped out and came running into the store. He was wearing a wet t-shirt and wet board shorts, and his wet bare feet were full of sand. As he came running in, his hair all messed up, he said, *"Theo, leave now. Go home, get your surfboard, come straight to the beach,"* and told me which beach he was at. *"The surf is awesome,"* he shouted.

I was trying to tell him I had to work until one o'clock because it was Saturday, but I was talking to his back because he was running out of the door. He didn't even shake my hand. I walked after him, but by the time I got to the door, he was in his car speeding off. I stood on the pavement and watched him drive off into the distance back to the beach. All of a sudden I decided I did not like my job anymore! I worked until one o'clock, then I went home, got my surfboard and went to the beach.

The next day, Sunday, I decided, *"I'm going to pray and ask God for a new job where I don't have to work on Saturdays."* I took a card, a five by three inch card, which was blank on both sides. I decided to think carefully about what I wanted as far as this new job was concerned. The first thing I wrote on the card was, **Number one: I want a five-day week job**. After all, that was the reason for the prayer, not to work on Saturdays. Then I thought, *"What kind of work do I want to do?"* I felt like I had served my time working in one store and I needed to be out on the road. I needed a selling job where I could get out and see the scenery. Repping to different retailers would be great, a little bit of scenery while I worked would be nice.

I wrote on the card: **Number two: I want a repping job.** I wanted to be a representative of a company, selling products.

Then I decided: **Number three. I wanted to be the manager of my department.** So I wrote, 'I want to be the manager.'

Number four. I needed to earn at least R600 a month, basic salary. At that time, in 1975, I could buy between $1.15 and $1.20 with a Rand. The Rand was more valuable than a dollar in those days, so R600 would be a good basic salary. A basic salary means whether you sell anything or not, you get R600 at the end of the month. If you go on vacation you get R600 at the end of the month.

The fifth thing I wrote was, 'I want to earn at least R800 a month commission on top of the R600 basic.' I knew that I would sell better than the average salesman, so therefore I expected to earn R1200 to R1500 commission. But I wanted a structure that would guarantee me at least R800 a month commission.

At the time I was earning R1000 a month selling furniture, and I was the top salesman in the entire organization. I would win the monthly financial prize every month. At the beginning of the month when they gave out the prize I would say to all the salesmen and the sales manager, *"I'm going to win the prize next month too."*

The manager would say, *"Well, you probably will."*
I would say, *"Yes and if any two agree, it is done."*
The others would ask, *"When are we going to have a turn?"*
And I'd say, *"Never."* They also agreed then that I'd win it! So I'd confess it to them and I won. I used to count that prize money into my budget!

I was earning R1000 a month selling furniture, and now I was going to get R600 basic and at **least** R800 commission, giving me a total of R1400, which was a nice increase. I decided I also wanted a company car, because I didn't want to put wear and tear on my own car if I was going to be selling company products around town.

I wrote: **Number six, 'I need a company car.'** At that time, Datsun, which is now Nissan, was winning all the cross-country rally races, and a yellow one would be exciting. If I had a yellow 1600 Datsun (Nissan) I would be happy. So that's what I wrote on my card: **a yellow 1600 Datsun**.

Then I thought, *"When would I like to start my new job?"* This was the beginning of November, and November and December were very big months in the furniture industry. You would always earn at least twice as much as you would during a normal month, because folks came to buy furniture at that time of the year. I decided I wanted to start my new job on January 1st when the sales frenzy was over.

So I wrote on my card: **Number seven, 'I will start working at my new job on the first of January 1976.'**

I have done this same thing over and over many times since then, so I can assure you, this principle will work no matter what it is you're asking God for. If you are asking God for the salvation of family members, if you are asking God for personal health, whatever it is, this principle will work for you because if you ask in faith, you will receive it.

Then I turned the card over and wrote on the other side, four scriptures that really encouraged my faith. I have used these same four scriptures through the years, to believe God for many different things.

There have been times I have looked at one verse of scripture for over half an hour. I remember one particular time I was attacked because of a serious financial challenge I faced. I was cold with sweat from the absolute fear I faced.I closed the door, shut myself in, found a scripture that answered my need and I meditated on that verse for over half an hour. I went from fear into faith, into peace, into rejoicing. I came out of there excited on the inside. Had the circumstances changed? No, but I was pumped up on the inside, full of confidence, ready to go and face my Goliath. My faith **did** change the circumstances.

It's really important that we meditate on the word before we pray. Don't rush into prayer. Whenever you're going to pray about anything, always take out your Bible, find a verse that says you can have it, and then read it for a while; allow that to build your faith, then you pray.

It's really important that we meditate on the word
before we pray.
Don't rush into prayer.

Mark 11:23 (NKJ) *For assuredly, I say to you, whoever says to this mountain, "Be removed and be cast into the sea," and does not doubt in his heart, but believes that those things he says will be done, he will have whatever he says.*

It's very important for us to seek first the kingdom of God. When we pray and believe for things, let's believe for His kingdom to go forward in the earth and expand. That's imperative. If you will seek first the kingdom, the rest will be added to you, Jesus said. However, some people have this idea, or the devil has lied to them, that you cannot pray for anything personal, any of your own needs or desires. You only have to pray for things that would help someone get saved and further the kingdom of God. That would be first prize and that would be most important, priority number one. However, look at this verse; the Lord Jesus said, *"whoever says will have whatever he says."* Another lie the devil tell us is, 'You know it's no good making bold positive confessions of your faith for the things you need, because you're not living a squeaky clean Christian life, you're not a super saint. When you become a super saint, then you can make positive confessions, and it will work for you. But until that time, you must admit your confessions are not going to work, because you're not up there spiritually where you'd like to be.' May I point out that Jesus said, '***whoever*** *says, will have whatever he says if he believes what he says*' (**Mark 11:23**). That means whether the person is a Christian, a God lover, a heathen, or a God hater — he's in the category of 'whoever'. If he says something and believes it, it's going happen. Jesus said, *"The good man out of the good treasure of his heart brings forth the good things. And the evil man out of the evil treasure of his heart brings forth the evil things"* (**Luke 6:45**). The point I'm making is this: you don't have to be a super Christian for this to work for you. You could be fumbling and faltering, stumbling and falling; as long as you get up and keep trying, trust in God to improve, you can use these principles and they will work for you, whether you are a ten out of ten super saint, or a one out of ten struggling to get up saint.

I'm not trying to tell people they can live a bad life and still make it. Don't get me wrong. I'm not saying live like the devil, and you will still go to heaven. That's a lie. Anybody who believes they can live like the devil and go to heaven is mistaken. That is a lie from the devil. I want you to know that if you make a mistake, your faith is still going to work for you. The word '***believe***' is mentioned one time, '***say***' is mentioned three times. There is three times more emphasis made on saying than there is on believing in that verse.

Say this, *"I have to make sure I start saying what I believe. I've got to focus three times more on my saying than I do on my believing."* Believing is a result of saying and meditating in the word.

> **Mark 11:24 *(NKJ)*** *Therefore I say to you, whatever things you ask when you pray, believe that you receive them, and you will have them.*

> **John 16:23 *(NKJ)*** …***Most assuredly***, *I say to you, whatever you ask the Father in my name **He will give you**.'*

The correct procedure for prayer that gets answered is to ask the Father using the name of Jesus. If Bill Gates gives you a check for ten thousand dollars, you go to the bank, give the teller the check and they give you the money. They don't interrogate you, and ask you a bunch of questions. They just look at the signature on the bottom of the check, they see Bill Gates' name there and give you the money. Likewise, when you use the name of Jesus, the Father says, *"Look at the name at the bottom of that check. It's Jesus,"* and you receive what you ask for. It's not your goodness (although it's important) that gets your prayer answered, it's the name of Jesus — the authority of that name and all the Lord Jesus did for us at Calvary. That's why the Father answers your prayer. We say, *"I'm not using my name Father, I'm not coming in my qualifications, or how good I am. I'm asking for this in the name of Jesus."*

Jesus could have said, *"Ask and you will receive if it's extremely important."* He could have said, *"Ask and you will receive if it is a matter of life and death."* But He didn't say that. He said, *"Ask and you will receive that your joy may be full."*

Say this, *"God wants me to be happy, and if things aren't right and I'm not happy, He told me to ask for what I need so I can be happy."*

> **Mark 11:24 (KJ)** *Therefore I say unto you, what things soever ye desire. . .*

I've heard it preached that God will meet your needs but He won't meet your greed. That was a title of the sermon that took 45 minutes to preach and I had to endure through that message. It didn't persuade me because it arrived too late, I had already seen God answer prayers, and found out for myself that He'll meet my desires too. He said, *"whatever things you desire,"* not only need. **"When** *you pray…"* *put a circle around that in your Bible. That's the key, that's the answer.* **"When"** refers to time. When you pray, at that time of prayer, we must do something. What is it we must do? *"Believe you receive them."* What do you receive? The thing you desire.

What did I desire? A new job. I had the whole list on my card, and I had the four scriptures written on the other side (**Mark 11:23-24 NKJ**; **John 16:23-24 NKJ**). The thing I desired was this new job and so I proceeded to read off the card to the Father. I said, *"Father I come to you in the name of the Lord Jesus and I ask you for a new job."* Before I prayed that prayer, I knelt. You don't have to kneel, you can sit. In

Acts 2, 120 people received the Holy Spirit in the Upper Room and spoke in tongues and the Bible says they were all sitting down. They weren't kneeling, they were all sitting. That was a very holy moment. God knows if we respect and honor Him within our hearts. Nevertheless, I was kneeling. I took out my card and I read those four scriptures over a number of times, out loud to myself. I didn't shout them, just read them. *"Whatever you ask the Father in my name, He'll give you. Ask and you will receive that your joy may be full."* That's how I read them out for about 10 minutes or so. The more I read them, the more excited I got until I knew that this impossible prayer would be answered. I stopped reasoning about this. I started going by how I sensed this was working in my heart. I stopped reasoning about the impossibility of it. Then I said, *"Father, I come to you in the name of Jesus."* And held up my card. *"Father, I ask you for this job in the name of Jesus,"* and I read off those things one at a time. *"I ask you for a five day a week job. I ask you that it would be a repping job. I ask you that I'd be the manager. I ask you for $600 a month basic salary, more than $800 commission, a brand new yellow Datsun 1600 and that I would start working on January 1st 1976. In the name of Jesus."* I asked Him for the seven items I had listed, on my card. Then I said, *"The Lord Jesus said when I pray I must believe I receive it."* So I said, *"Father I believe you hear my prayer and I believe you grant me this request. I believe you're taking care of this right now. I believe you are answering my prayer right now. I believe therefore that I receive this job **now** in the name of Jesus. I thank you because I believe you **have** answered my prayer."*

It is only good manners to say thank you. So I said, *"Father, I want to thank you for answering my prayer."* I began to praise God and from then on 80% of my communication with the Father about that job was praise and worship. I'll show you how I did it. I said, *"Father I want to thank you for answering my prayer in the name of Jesus. I thank you for giving me this wonderful job. Father I want to thank you, I worship you for my new job. Praise you for my new job. I lift my hands and praise you and worship you for my new job."* Why? Because I believed I received it when I prayed. I said, *"**I believe I have it now**."*

That is important. I never asked God to give me the new job on January 1st 1976. No — I asked Him to give it to me when I prayed. I received the job at the time of prayer; it is therefore my job the moment I stop praying. I will begin working on the first day of January. In my mind I imagined an office somewhere with a desk, and my name on it. In my mind I saw that. Somewhere I have a job. It's mine now.

If we are asking the Lord for money — let's say we need $1,000 really urgently and we pray this way for the money, for us to then think, *"I wonder how God's going to get it to me? Perhaps God's going to send it with the postman? Yes, when I open the post in the morning, perhaps there'll be $1,000 check in there. Or maybe the taxman is going to give me $1,000 back next week. Or maybe I'm getting a refund. Or maybe…"* If you think like that, then guess what, you **did not** receive it, **you don't believe you have it. You are still waiting for it to come.**

We have got to **believe we receive** what we ask for when we pray. We've got to believe at that moment it becomes ours. If it is $1,000, or $10,000 you must believe you have **got it** in your **wallet**, in your **pocket**, or in your **bank** once you have finished praying and say, *"Amen"*. If it's a job, I have to believe I have the job right then and there. It's **my** job, and I have it **now**.

> We have to believe we receive what we ask for when we pray.

I am **now** employed by a brand new company but I have no clue who it is! My part is to **believe** I receive it, that I **have it now**, once I have finished praying. God's part is the, "**shall have them.**" If I start thinking about how God's going to do the *"shall have them"*, I'm out of faith and I'm meddling in God's part of the arrangement. I'm not to meddle with God's part. He is well able to take care of His part. I'm only supposed to take care of my part. So I believed I received it and I got up off my knees and walked away. **What I'm sharing with you here is extremely important**. I walked away and looked at the place where I was kneeling and said, *"Father, five minutes ago at that moment when I prayed, I received a new job. So for the last five minutes I have been the proud employee of this wonderful new job."*

Then I started telling God what I got, *"I've **got** this wonderful job,"* and I mentioned the seven things I received, and I worshipped Him again. I said, *"Father, I want to worship you. Thank you for this wonderful job you gave me ten minutes ago."*

On Monday morning when I woke up, the first thing I did was grab my card next to my bed. I looked at those scriptures, so the devil couldn't put any doubt in my mind. I filled my heart again with those scriptures. Lying in bed I raised my hands. *"Thank you Father for this wonderful job. This job I received yesterday at this time. Oh, thank you for this job that I have had for the last day. Praise God."* I spent time thanking God for each of the seven items He had given me.

> **Mark 11:23 (NKJ)** *For assuredly, I say to you, whoever says to this mountain, 'Be removed and be cast into the sea,' and does not doubt in his heart, but believes that those things he says will be done, he will have whatever he says.*

I had to do some more 'saysing.' I had to do a lot more saying. I'm believing, but I've got to say it. I got into the office that morning and I had 17 other salesmen to talk to! It's big news when somebody resigns. So I sneaked up to the first one and whispered to him, *"Can I tell you a secret?"*
"Sure, what?"
I said, *"Shhh, don't tell anybody."*
"Okay."

"I'm resigning."

"What? Why are you resigning?"

"I have got this amazing job. I got it yesterday." I waited because I knew he was going to ask me about it. So he said, *"Tell me about it."*

"Sure," I said, and I started telling him about the seven things on my list. I don't think I finished before he said to me, *"Where is this job?"*

I was taken by surprise, I actually did not think about how I would answer a question like that. And I didn't have a clue where my job was! I thought fast because I'm not going to confess I don't know where it is. So I said, *"It's a secret, I'm not telling you where it is."*

Then he asked, *"Are there any more vacancies?"*

I said, *"No. Only one and I got it."*

He said, *"Oh. If any more come up, will you let me know?"*

I said, *"Sure I will."*

Do you know what I noticed when I finished making that confession? My faith went up to a higher level. Abraham became fully persuaded in **Romans 4:17-22**, and after saying that, I became more persuaded, more convinced, and more faith rose in my heart.

Amazingly enough, we think we're in faith, and we are, but we can have more faith than we have right now. Our faith is unlimited because we can have as much faith as God has. **Mark 11:22** says, *"Have the faith of God."* In other words, 'have the God kind of faith.' God can increase our faith through His word. Think about Moses parting the Red Sea, or bringing billions of gallons of water out of a rock, to meet the needs of three million people and all their animals. Think about Joshua who stopped the sun in the sky for about 23 hours. Or think about the prophet Isaiah, who turned the sundial back 10 degrees when he prayed for King Hezekiah (**2 Kings 20:9-11**).

Yes we can have much more faith than we have at the moment, however, remember, just a mustard seed is enough to get the job done. So don't fear. If you have only a little, that is enough. Just put it to work. Just turn your faith loose. *"How do I do that, Pastor Theo?"* Follow the instructions you are learning in this book, understand the power of your words when you speak God's word. Jesus said in **Matthew 19:26**, *"With God **all things** are possible."* In **Mark 9:23** Jesus said, *"**All things** are possible to him who believes."*

So I noticed my faith grew and I was excited. The next day I found another salesman, and did the same thing. I did the same thing for seventeen days. Then when that was all done, I started out with the first salesman again. I said, *"Did I tell you about my new job?"*
He said, *"Yes."*
I asked *"Do you mind if I tell you about it again?"*
I had to say it. I had to talk about it. Any time the devil tried to put any doubt in my mind, I'd find somebody I could tell.

When we have ministered to folks and they get healed, I tell them, *"If the devil tries to come back, if at any time you feel any symptoms come back — pick up the phone. Phone some-*

body and tell them that Jesus **healed** *you, tell them what Jesus did for you, and the pain will just leave."*

I repeated the contents of my card every day. The end of the month came, and the devil shot a big arrow of doubt into my head. He said, *"How are you going to get this job when you haven't even been for one interview? You haven't even read one newspaper."* I hadn't opened up one newspaper, imagine that? I'm confessing I've got this job, but I haven't read one newspaper to find a vacancy. I had not told people I was looking for a job; no one knew I was looking for a job. The only ones I spoke to thought I had one. The devil said, *"You're crazy. You are **not** getting a job. You know you are crazy. You have not even looked in a newspaper."* He was trying to get me to think I had to open a newspaper. If I did that when I had already got my job, what would happen then? Imagine if I got a newspaper and said, *"Let me see."* I would have blown it, because I believed I had a job already. Why go look for a job when I already had one? I was going to start work at my new employment come January 1st 1976.

Say this, *"My actions need to be in line with my words. Otherwise my actions can contradict my words."* We can say we believe it, but **our actions can prove we don't believe it**. We have to be careful how we act.

When he said that to me, at first it threw me, so I ran upstairs to the restroom, and closed the door. **I never said one word**. I took out my card, read those scriptures again and then I said, *"Mr. Devil,* **I already have the job**. *Look,* **here is my evidence**. *Whatever things you desire* **when** *you pray,* **I have done that**, *therefore I have it. It's my job."*

We can say we believe something, but our actions can prove we don't believe. We have to be careful of how we act.

Halfway through the month of December, an interesting thing happened which really helped me. It didn't dawn on me what happened until it was over. I was standing at the front of the store waiting for clients to come in. A man came in and said, *"I'm looking for a fridge. It needs to be so many feet high, so many square feet big."*

I said, *"Yeah, I've got the exact one. Barlow's, right? A Leonard?"* He said, *"That's the one I want."* I took him to it and he confirmed it was the right one. Our company Beares, would give us R20 ($24) for selling that particular fridge. But the manufacturer would give us an additional R50 ($60) for selling it. Therefore we would earn a total of R70 ($84) for selling that large fridge. Back in those days that was a lot of money. The gentleman said, *"I don't have the money now, but next month, in January, I will come in and buy it."*

Immediately without thinking, I said, *"I won't be here, I've got a new job. I'm actually leaving on the first of January but I will introduce you to a salesman who's a friend of mine. He can help you when you come back to buy the fridge in January."*

After that event, it dawned on me, that without even think-ing about it, my heart had taken charge and my action was a result of the fact that I was in faith. If there had been any doubt in my heart, I would have said, *"Hey, R70! Okay, I'll keep this deal. Come back and see me. Here's my card. I'll phone you next month."* If I had done that, without realizing it I would have lost my new job, because of that act of unbelief. I could have thought, *"I'll phone him from my new job once I get it, and tell him to go and see another salesman. So just in case, I'll keep it for me."* No! That would have been an action that tells me I'm not in faith. But I didn't even think about it. Only after the event did I realize I was in complete faith. My actions proved it.

So, now the end of the month came, and just before Christmas, the devil shot another arrow and said, *"If you've got a job like this, why don't you resign? Prove you've got a job and resign."* So I took out my card, ran upstairs, closed the restroom door, read the scriptures and said, *"Mr. Devil, here's the evidence I've got the job. It is* **Mark 11:24** *and* **John 16:23** *and* **24**. *I don't have to resign to prove I have it. I've got the words of Jesus to prove I have it."*

On the last day of December the store closed at midday and I went home. On New Year's Day, January 1, 1976, I went surfing. I was supposed to start work on New Year's Day, but it was a holiday. Back in 1976 in South Africa noth-ing happened on New Year's Day. Everything was closed down. When I prayed earlier on that year, I did not think about New Year's Day being a holiday. Of course I knew it, but it did not dawn on me at the time. So I went surfing. I thought, *"Well, we've got the day off, praise the Lord. I'm going surfing."* I came home at three o'clock. On my door was a little note. *"Phone Mike Oosthuis, urgent."* So I phoned Mike. I knew who he was, a good Christian businessman, he wasn't a personal friend but an acquaintance. I said, *"Hi Mike, how are you doing?"*

"Yeah, great," he said. *"Look, our salesman resigned yesterday and we need to replace him. I've heard you're a good salesman. I'd like for you to come for an interview, would you do that?"*

I said, *"Sure, let me have a shower and I'll come on over."*

He said, *"No, come as you are."*

I said, *"No Mike, I am wet. I have just come from the beach. My t-shirt is wet, my board shorts are wet, I have nothing on my feet. I have beach sand all over me, my hair is a mess, I look a wreck. I'm not dressed for a job interview."*

He said, *"Please come as you are. Mike Taylor (the other director) and I have been waiting all day for you to phone. We came in this morning; we put that note on your door this morning. It is New Year's Day and we have waited here all day in case you phoned. Please come over right now. We want to go home to our families."*

It's a holiday. Of course they want to go home. I went on over and as I drove I thought, *"Isn't this amazing? Sam Stark was dressed exactly the same way I'm dressed now when I decided to pray for this job!"*

I haven't heard of anybody in all the world going for an interview with seawater all over them, wet t-shirt, wet board shorts, and barefoot. I have never heard of that, but it happened to me. I arrived and Mike showed me what they sold. They manufactured precast concrete products for the building industry and roads. He asked, *"Can you sell all this?"*

I said, *"No problem."*

He asked, '*Have you thought about what kind of salary you would like?*'

"Yeah, as a matter of interest, I have," I said.

He took out his pen and I started telling him everything that was on my card — going down the list: one, two, three, four, five, six. He was shocked that I had all that at my fingertips. Then he frowned and said, *"We have **never, ever** paid **anybody** this kind of money."*

So I said, *"Mike, this is a small business and you can't afford the luxury of an inexperienced salesman. You have to have the best, and that's me. God is on my side Mike. I will do better than any salesman you have ever had before."*

He said, *"Okay, when do you want to start?"*

I said, *"Right now."*

"Right now?"

"Yes."

"Okay, I'll pay you from today. Will you be working tomorrow?" I said, *"No, I've got to go and resign at Beares."*

The following morning I handed in my resignation at Beares. They wanted me to work 30 days notice, then they said, *"Where are you going to work next?"* I said, *"It is a secret."* They said, *"You can go now, we will pay you for the next 30 days, but we want you to go now."*

From there I went to pick up my yellow Datsun (Nissan). The dealership said they did not have a 1600, they had stopped manufacturing them, and they only had 1800s. That was a brand new model that had just come in, a lot nicer. I phoned Mike. *"Mike, sad news, no 1600's, but don't worry, they've got 1800's."*

"How much more?" he asked. I told him. He said, *"Okay, get it."* So I drove out with a brand new 1800 yellow Datsun.

Anyway, now think about this. The man working at Taydee Pre-Cast Concrete resigned his job the day before, and God gave him a better job, with more money. Those two directors had no intention of working on New Year's Day until the day before, when their salesman resigned. They had to go to work on New Year's Day to interview me. Those two directors were blessed and benefitted by me joining, and I was blessed and benefitted by a lot more money. Everybody won. **But think about how God rearranged their lives so that my prayer could be answered**. He ordered their steps without them realizing it. They had no idea that God was directing them to go to work that day. They didn't realize, sitting there all day, that they were doing that because God had told them to do it. The man who resigned and got a better job, accepted that job not knowing that God was telling him to accept that job. God moved a whole bunch of people around without them even knowing it because I was trusting Him.

It is totally awesome what God will do for His children, if we will dare to trust Him. '**The Power of Positive Words**.'

195

Say this, *"If I believe God, He will arrange people, circumstances, and events, in order for me to receive what I am trusting Him for. He is the God of the supernatural. A miraculous God, who answers prayer. Thank you Jesus."*

> If I believe God, He will arrange people,
> circumstances, and events, in order for me to
> receive what I am trusting Him for

Now think of those seven things that came together on the exact day. It wasn't a regular working day, it was a holiday. That had to be a miracle.

Chapter Eleven

The Joshua Principle

Proverbs 18:14 (NKJ) *A man's spirit sustains him in sickness, but a crushed spirit who can bear?*

The spirit of man will sustain him in sickness. The word 'spirit' could also mean heart. So, your spirit will sustain you in a time of sickness. Or, you might say, your spirit man will sustain you in a time of trial, temptation, problems, family challenges, financial need, whatever it might be. Your spirit man will sustain you in that circumstance.

What does it mean when the Bible says sustain, what can we expect to happen? What does that word mean?

The word in the Hebrew is **K-U-W-L,** pronounced **Kool,** This word means 'to keep'. Therefore your spirit, your heart, will keep you in a time of challenge. The word also means, 'to maintain'. Your heart will maintain you through your challenge. It also means, 'to guide'. That means your heart will guide you through your challenge. You see, your heart is in fellowship with God who knows all things, who sees all things. We're limited by the five senses to our natural circumstances, but God is not. He knows everything, He knows the big picture and He will guide you through the challenges of life with least resistance, and bring you to people who will help you. God wants to guide you. Your heart, like a homing pigeon, will lead you where you should go to find victory. Another word to explain this word 'sustain' is the word 'nourish'. Your heart will nourish you in that time, or make provision for you.

Now this scripture could have said God will do all that for you, and we know God does. But it didn't say that. It said, 'your heart will', or 'your spirit man will'. In other words, your heart, which is in fellowship with God, will receive that strength from God and that strength from God will guide you and strengthen you. So keep feeding your heart on something that will build your faith and all this will happen. Hope will return.

> **Proverbs 4:23 (NLT)** *Above all else guard your heart for it affects everything you do.*

God said, *"Above all else guard your heart for it affects everything you do."* This means, if our heart is filled with faith, and a challenge comes over the horizon unexpectedly, our heart will say the right thing at the right moment. Just like when Jesus stood up on the boat in the Sea of Galilee and spoke to the storm, and suddenly there came a great calm. The wind ceased and the water was still, so you will speak and calm the storms of your life, using Christ's authority released through words of faith. You will speak in His place, on His behalf.

> **Ephesians 1:22 (NLT)** *says, God has put all things under the authority of Christ, and gave Christ this authority for the benefit of the church.*

All that God did for Christ, and all God did to Christ in His resurrection, God did for man, the born-again, new creation man. Therefore this authority of Christ is for our benefit, to enforce the victory Christ won for us at Calvary. To speak in His place and command His plans to be fulfilled in this world. Such is the power of our words. A few people in time past understood this, like Joshua, Moses, Isaiah, David, Abraham, Paul the Apostle and others. As we meditate on these truths, I believe God will raise up an army of spiritual giants to face the storms of life in these end times. We are the conquerors for this hour. You were born for such a time as this. We won't have to stop and think, 'Well what do I do now?' Our heart will respond and take charge. It is vital that our hearts are ready for any emergency. Like a karate expert that's highly trained, if anybody jumps out at him in the dark night, he's ready. We have to be that way in our heart. We don't want to be filled with doubt, unbelief and fear, because when those problems come, we're going to say the wrong thing.

If you've done all to stand, begin to rest and just simply feed your heart on faith food. A great example of what we are discussing here is Joshua and the instructions God gave to him when he was about to take over from Moses. Moses was called of God to take three million Israelites from Egypt to the promised land of Canaan, the land of

199

milk and honey. Then he died and Joshua was commissioned to take over from Moses. Joshua had a very challenging task because he had seen Moses part the Red Sea, he had seen Moses bring the plagues down, he had seen bread, manna, fall from the sky under Moses' leadership. He had seen thousands upon thousands of quail fly into the camp of Israel and say, 'eat me'. He had seen water come out of a rock, enough for three million people and their animals. Joshua had a tough act to follow — Amen?

God gave Joshua a formula, if you would, a principle that he could follow that would make him successful, because God didn't want Joshua to fail. God wanted the children of Israel to get to the Promised Land. He knew that Joshua needed help because the Israelites weren't the most accommodating and cooperative bunch of people. They were world champion complainers.

> **Joshua 1:2 (NKJ)** *'Moses my servant is dead. Now then, you and all these people, get ready to cross the Jordan River into the land I am about to give to them—to the Israelites.*

The children of Israel were camped on the east side of the Jordan River, and God said, *"Joshua, I want you to go over the Jordan River, go west into the heart of the promised land that I have given you."*

> **Joshua 1:3 (NKJ)** *I will give you every place where you set foot, as I promised Moses.*

> [4] *Your territory will extend from the desert to*
> *Lebanon, and from the great river, the Euphrates—*
> *all the Hittite country—to the Great Sea on the west.*

They were standing on the south side of Lebanon looking north. God said, *"All the way up to the River Euphrates,"* (which is in fact, almost all of Syria). "All the land of the Hittites, (which is now Jordan), and to the great sea towards the going down of the sun, (which is the Mediterranean Sea on the west). That's a huge vast expanse of land that God said was theirs. Why did He say that? God made that covenant with Abraham and **his seed** (**Christ**). Whenever the Bible talks about **seed singular**, as in Abraham's seed, **it's referring to Christ**, a descendent of Abraham through the ages. When it talks about descendants plural, it is referring to everyone who is a descendent of Abraham.

There was a covenant made between God and Abraham; and of course between God and Jesus. This covenant between Abraham and Jesus with the Father is in place, and is still functioning. The Lord Jesus operated under the Abrahamic Covenant when He was on the earth. We must understand this covenant was fully ratified, enforced, when God made this promise to give that land to Abraham and Christ. As far as God is concerned it belongs to them today.

> **Galatians 3:16 (NKJ) Now to Abraham and**
> **his Seed were the promises made.** *He does not*
> *say, "And to seeds," as of many, but as of one, "And*
> *to your Seed,"* **who is Christ.**

Genesis 12:7 (KJ) *And the Lord appeared unto Abram, and said, Unto thy* **seed** *will I give this land:*

Genesis 13:15 (KJ) *For all the land which thou seest, to thee will I give it, and to thy* **seed** *for ever.*

Genesis 15:18 (KJ) ...**the Lord made a covenant with Abram, saying, Unto thy seed have I given this land**, *from the river of Egypt (Nile) unto the great river, the river Euphrates:*

19 The Kenites, and the Kenizzites, and the Kadmonites,

20 And the Hittites, and the Perizzites, and the Rephaims,

21 And the Amorites, and the Canaanites, and the Girgashites, and the Jebusites.

According to the Bible account, all that land belongs to Abraham and Christ. Whether you believe the Bible or not is up to you. I believe that land is theirs, and one day in the future they will own it all, and use it all. Israel disobeyed God, they turned from God, so they lost the inheritance and were scattered throughout the nations of the earth. As the time of the Gentiles is drawing to a close, God is bringing Israel back into the land He gave to Abraham and Christ. The moment Jesus begins His reign from Jerusalem, at that moment, the land mentioned in **Genesis 15:18-21** will belong to Christ. It will all be part of Israel's borders.

> **Joshua 1:5 (NKJ)** *No one will be able to stand up against you all the days of your life. As I was with Moses, so I will be with you; I will never leave you nor forsake you.*
>
> *⁶ 'Be strong and courageous, because you will lead these people to inherit the land I swore to their forefathers to give them.*

Note God said to Joshua, *"I swore to Abraham, Isaac and Jacob to give them this land, and you, Joshua, will divide it among the twelve tribes."* For those who think God might be done with Israel, please read **Romans 11** and you will find that God is not finished with Israel. They're going to come back into their inheritance. But here you see clearly, *"I swore to give them this land."*

> **Joshua 1:7 (NKJ)** *Only be strong and very courageous,* **that you may observe to do** *according to all that the law that my servant Moses commanded you and do not turn from it to the right or to the left* **that you may prosper wherever you go**.

God said to Joshua, '**If you will do the first five books of the Bible**, *which Moses wrote,* **you'll prosper in everything you do**.' Let's stop and reflect on that for a moment. God has given Joshua a huge task, and God is desperately desirous of Joshua succeeding. He can't allow Joshua to fail. If Joshua is going to walk in Moses' footsteps, he will need to be respected by the people the way they respected Moses.

God is giving Joshua a principle to make this happen. If that principle worked for Joshua, to help him with that huge challenge, then surely this principle is going to work for us, in our comparatively minor challenges. We ought to heed what God said to Joshua. I believe there's a lot of valuable information here for us today. Here is the formula of success that God gave to Joshua.

> **Joshua 1:8 (NKJ)** *This Book of the Law shall not depart from your mouth, but you shall meditate in it day and night, that you may observe to do according to all that is written in it. For then you will make your way prosperous, and then you will have good success.*

God told Joshua, *"If **you** do this you will make **your way** prosperous."* He didn't say, 'Joshua, **I** will make you prosperous.'

God has already provided everything we need for prosperity and success for this life through Calvary. God's done His part. He's given all He can give. He gave His life. What more can He give? Now it's up to us to seize the opportunity and take dominion, or you might say, take advantage of what God has given us. Here's the formula, He said, *"Meditate in the word of God day and night. If you do that, Joshua, it will come out your mouth."* Did the Lord Jesus not say, *"**The good man out of the good treasure of his heart brings forth good things**. And the evil man brings forth evil things."* Which means whatever your heart is full of will come out your mouth. So if our heart is filled with God's word it will come out of our mouth. And then what? It directs our circumstances. You'll make your way prosperous.

Say that, *"The principle is to meditate on the word continually so that at the right time, whatever the circumstances, the word of God, and positive things, will come out of my mouth and cause me to succeed."*

That's the principle. It's repeated over and over in the Bible. Jesus taught it, and we need to understand that's what God gave to Joshua for his success. You might think, 'I've got no strength to even say anything.' That's fine, just listen to faith teachings, and meditate in the word of God. Sooner or later your heart will be pumped up, encouraged, and you'll start speaking out boldly without even realizing what you're doing.

Meditate on the word continually so that at the right time, whatever the circumstances, the word of God and positive things, will come out of your mouth and cause you to succeed.

Joshua 1:9 (NKJ) *Have I not commanded you? Be strong and of good courage; do not be afraid, nor be dismayed, for the Lord your God is with you wherever you go.'*

God gave Joshua an instruction. He said, *"Meditate on the word and you will be full of faith, courage and fear will melt away."*

Joshua was leading the Israelites in battle against the Amorites. Joshua and the Israelites got the upper hand in this battle and night was beginning to fall. They needed more daylight to ensure victory, or the enemy would escape at nightfall and regroup by the next morning. They did not want to start all over again the next day. So Joshua did something spectacular, to say the least.

> **Joshua 10:12 (NKJ)** *Then Joshua spoke to the Lord in the day when the Lord delivered up the Amorites before the children of Israel, and he (Joshua) said in the sight of Israel:* **'Sun stand still over Gibeon and moon in the valley of Aijalon.'**
>
> [13] **So the sun stood still and the moon stopped**, *till the people had revenge on their enemies.*
>
> [14] *And there has been no day like that, before it or after it,* **that the Lord heeded the voice of a man...**

How awesome is that? Joshua meditated in God's word until his heart was full of faith. Then in the heat of the battle, Joshua shouts out loud to the sun in the sky, 'Sun stand still over Gibeon and moon in the valley of Aijalon.' God instantly responds to the faith of the man, how awesome!

There is a man by the name of Harold Hill who wrote a book. In it he describes how he used to work for NASA. They were encountering challenges when they were trying to land a man on the moon, because there seemed to be a day missing in time past. Mr. Hill brought this to the attention of the other scientists working with him, and they discovered that this story of Joshua accounted for 23 missing hours. The other missing hour was found in the story of Hezekiah's sundial moving backwards ten degrees when Isaiah prayed in **2 Kings 20:9-11**. NASA was able to re-calculate everything and the mission was successful, landing a man on the moon. He also describes in his book how that NASA has since then said he never worked there and denied that this ever happened. We will probably never be able to prove who is telling the truth between NASA and Mr. Hill. After reading what Mr. Hill said, I believe that he was telling the truth. Even if we disregard Mr. Hill's account altogether, let us examine the Bible because we know the Bible is correct. Try and find Mr. Hill's book, it is out of print. It is a very interesting read. Nevertheless, the sun stopped for 23 hours, or about a whole day, and then Hezekiah made up the rest.

The earth is 24,900 miles in circumference and it rotates every 24 hours, that means it's traveling at approximately 1,000 miles per hour. We are moving at 1,000 miles per hour in a circle and we are also moving around the sun. The moon orbits around the earth. Joshua spoke to the sun and the moon and said, *"Stop."* The earth stopped instantly when Joshua spoke, and no one fell off the planet, no one even fell over. Those soldiers fighting didn't even know that anything was different. But they were going 1,000 miles an hour and like you hit a brick wall they stopped, and no one was aware of it. The oceans didn't run over the land, nothing changed. God is God. When Joshua said that, God calculated everything in a split second and did it for him. Isn't that amazing? And then, when it started up again, no one knew. From zero to 1,000 miles per hour, in one second or less. That's quite some acceleration, and no one knew it. That is amazing, but what amazes me even more is that Joshua, in the heat of the battle would say to the sun and the moon, *"Stop. Stand still!"* Where did he get the authority and faith to do that? Where did he get the right to mess up God's creation? Where did Joshua get the faith to command the sun to stand in the sky? He was practicing what God told him to do. He was reading scripture day and night. It was so in his heart that when the moment arose, he took the opportunity and said what needed to be said to fix the problem.

It doesn't matter what the challenge might be, if our heart is full of faith, we will say the right thing at the right time, to ensure that victory is guaranteed. If we say we can't, we will never make it. *"We will never have the money; that person will never come to Jesus; they will never get healed; they are going to die."* If we talk like that all the time, God cannot help us, there's no faith in those statements. But if we say, *"I believe God can fix this problem. I believe Jesus can heal this person"*; if we will say the right thing, God can work through us and solve the problem just like He did for Joshua with the sun and the moon. And of course they conquered their enemies and won the battle.

Let's not spend all of our time trying to solve our problems by our natural means, stressing out, worrying, lying awake at night, and thinking about it. Rather get out of bed, open your Bible and start reading and meditating on the word of God. You know what will happen? Your heart will be encouraged, hope and faith will rise up in your heart, you will enter into peace, and you will sleep like a baby. It won't take more than a half an hour. It beats lying awake all night long. Or put on a faith teaching, and lie in bed and listen until you start snoring. I promise you one thing, if you listen to the word of God, you will be encouraged in your faith. Your heart will rise up and bring you out of your problem.

If I feed my heart on faith food my heart will rise up and deliver me.

Say this, *"If I feed my heart on faith food my heart will rise up and deliver me."*

In 1997 we were building a very large youth center, it cost millions of Rand. In those days the Rand was two to one. I could buy .50c with a R1. Five years before that I could buy $1.15 with a R1. An offer was made to help with the project that appeared to be from God. I accepted this offer without praying about it.

Say this, *"Not every open door is from the Lord. We must pray to see what God says first."*

Nevertheless, we went ahead. The wheels came off, we got into a hopeless mess, and at the end of the day we had to tear the building down and got into huge debt. It ended up in a court case. It hit the newspapers. Our members took some heat. The weaker Christians left the church.

We called every creditor and said, *"You can sue us for the money we owe you, and if you do, you will close us down and you will get nothing. But we guarantee you, if you will be patient with us, we will pay you every cent we owe at credit card interest rates,"* (which was somewhere between 23 and 28 percent), *"so consider this the best investment you have ever made with your money."* We paid everybody back over a period of three years. As a result the banks know that they can trust us because when we were against the ropes, in dire straits, we didn't run away. We faced the challenge, believed God and came out of it. Now banks trip over themselves to lend us money and we don't need to borrow any.

It was one of the darkest times of my life because we had to believe God to survive every day. The ship was level with the water. The smallest wave would have come into the boat and sunk it. In the natural it looked like the ministry was going to sink every day. So what did I do? I meditated in the word of God every day. I listened to faith tapes in my car, and at home when I was praying. I did that every day, two, three hours every day. My heart was filled with faith, hope and encouragement, and every time a new challenge came, I would speak from the abundance of my heart. I meditated in scriptures that promised us deliverance and financial provision. Of course I repented for my stupidity. God came through and delivered us. Even though I could not see the light at the end of the tunnel, God rescued us because my heart was filled with faith and I held fast to my confession. So, how did we overcome, how did all this happen? I believe the secret is just through feeding my faith. I put the principle that God gave to Joshua to work for me. **Don't ever underestimate the power of positive words**.

Sure, there have been times in my life when I felt like throwing in the towel and giving up. But it's at those times that I go to my Bible and read scriptures that build faith, until my heart is encouraged again. I won't open my door; I won't step out of my house, until I am ready to face the day.

Say this, *"God's word is the same today as it was for Joshua. If it worked for Joshua and gave him faith to conquer impossible challenges, God's word will do it for me. No matter how serious my problem may be, I can find courage, strength, faith and hope by reading the word of God. God will always come through. Praise God for the Joshua principle."*

Chapter Twelve

Applying the Power of Positive Words

In 1978 I had the opportunity of applying the Power of Positive Words. I was a Real Estate agent, selling houses and land for a living. I believed God for the job. I wrote down exactly what I wanted, prayed and asked God for it and He gave it to me. I did that four times in nine years. I received four different jobs in nine years, and each time I saw the Father give me exactly what I asked for. I have used my faith for many things before we even started in the full time ministry, and obviously many times since then.

The reason that I'm sharing experiences I had before we started the full time ministry is because people have this idea that God always answers the prayer of a full time minister, when the truth is that if we don't use faith, He won't answer our prayer whether we are in the full time ministry or not.

While I was selling homes I began to court Pastor Bev and asked her to marry me. I was trying to make a good impression on her. I stopped working and just took her out. We spent our days together and I was spending money everywhere. Of course, I ran out of money after a few months, and when you sell houses, you live on commission only. If you don't sell, you don't eat. Eventually my bank account was empty. All the money coming in from houses I had sold previously was used up. It was about that time that Bev agreed to marry me. There was a beautiful jewelry shop in the middle of Durban, and the owner was a personal friend of Bev's parents. They introduced me to the owner of the store on a Saturday morning. I was hopeful he would give me a good deal on Bev's engagement ring, because they were all friends.

I picked her up and took her to the store. She looked at all the jewelry in the store and there was nothing that she liked. She said to me, *"I don't like anything here."* I approached the owner and said, *"My girlfriend doesn't like any of the rings you've got on display. Is there any way you can help her?"*

He said, *"No problem, if she can sketch what she wants I can make it for her."*

She began drawing a beautiful ring on a piece of paper. He took the drawing and sat down with his calculator. After a few minutes he came back and said, *"I have a price."* Of course Bev and her parents were standing right there but he spoke to me privately so they couldn't hear what he was saying to me. He's showed me the numbers. Then he added, *"We are making this custom-made ring just for her, and if she doesn't like it, I will probably not be able sell it because other customers might not want a personally designed ring. That's why it's so expensive. If you want the ring, I will have to have cash in exchange for this ring."* Then he said, *"Do you want me to go ahead and make it for you?"*

Bev was looking at me with a big smile, and her parents were standing there, so I said, *"Sure!"* In the meantime I had no money at all. Nothing. Just enough money to fill the car with gas (petrol), and that was it. Fortunately I had a few groceries to eat. So when I said, *"Yes,"* I cannot tell you what was going through my head. I broke out in a cold sweat. The store was air-conditioned, it was cold in there, but I was perspiring. The sweat was running off my forehead and inside my shirt, and I thought, *"What have I got myself into?"* I had said yes because I wanted to impress her parents.

Let me back up. A little while before this, Bev had asked, *"Can you afford to marry me? And could you take care of me like my parents have taken care of me?"*
I said to her, *"Of course! What do you think?"* I said, *"You know my Father supplies all my needs according to His riches in glory in Christ Jesus."* I added, *"You'll never lack a day in your life."*
"Wow," she said, and went and told her parents, *"I have fallen into the butter with this guy, he is so rich."*
If only she knew! Anyhow, I had faith. You know if you have faith you've got anything you need. I had already believed God for four jobs so I knew how to use my faith.

When I said yes I knew what was required but my mind was racing. For me to have cash in fourteen days wasn't that easy, because **number one** — I had not worked for months, which meant I had no clients. I was totally out of touch with anybody who was interested in buying a home.

Number two — it takes three months from the time I sell a house for the red tape to take its course for me to get my check. The only way I was going to get immediate cash is if I sold a house on terms. That is like having a lease agreement for five years, and at the end of that time, the purchase comes into effect provided that the purchaser has saved sufficient money for a deposit. The purchaser has five years to save their deposit. Owners don't like selling their houses that way because they have to wait five years for their money. If they wanted to buy another house themselves, they might need the money to do so. Back in those days there weren't all that many options of moving forward without the cash coming out of your sale as there are today. As a result, we sold very few houses on terms, and in fact in the previous 18 months I was the only person who had sold a house on terms in the entire organization. I knew as I said 'yes', that I had to sell two houses on terms in fourteen days. I would have to do it twice in two weeks. As I said, I hadn't been working, I had no contacts, I didn't even know who wanted a house. I didn't even know which houses were still for sale. All the houses on the books were new to me. I would have to inspect all the new houses on the market. I was up a creek without an oar.

I said, *"Yes, certainly I will have the money in fourteen days,"* and they all heard me. I wasn't a good conversationalist that day! I couldn't wait to drop Bev off that Saturday night, and go home, and talk to God. I knew I had only one way out of this. If God didn't help me, I was sunk. Sunday morning came and I went to church. When I got home from church,

I was alone at home in my room. I said, *"Okay. I have to pray and seek God about this."* First thing I had to do was repent for not working. Why would that be? The Bible says if a man doesn't work, he shouldn't eat. Now if you don't have a job, believe God for one, but if you're just too lazy to work, then you have a problem, or if you're just running around, trying to impress ladies, you have another problem. That's exactly what I was doing. I impressed her so much I ran completely out of all my money.

I took my favorite scriptures for faith and I wrote them on the one side of a white card. Then I thought about what I wanted to ask the Father for. On the flip side of this card I wrote this prayer down. *"***Father I ask you in the name of Jesus to give me the sale of two houses on terms valued at more than x amount of Rand***."* I figured out how many houses I needed to sell, and what kind of commission I needed from the sale of those houses. Fortunately I was working in a wealthy part of the city and the houses were expensive, so I knew that **two** houses would pay for the ring. I also needed enough money to tithe on that income. I know the Hebrew word '**tithe**' means tenth, but I wanted to give God 20% instead of a tenth because I really wanted God to be excited about this deal. If I had no intention of giving the 20% to God after I got the money, God would know, and I would not have sold the houses. He knew I meant it and He knew I would keep my promise. So I said 20% for God and I knew that He would take notice of that! Then I needed enough money for a great evening dinner for the engagement that night. There was my list: Money for the ring, the tithe and a great dinner that night. Then I wrote, "**Father I thank you for hearing and answering my prayer, which I ask in the name of Jesus. I believe I receive this from you now in Jesus' name, I thank you it is done**."

Then I turned the card over and I read my four scriptures over and over, while kneeling at the foot of my bed. I read those scriptures out loud for about ten minutes. I was not shouting them out, but just reading them. I found as I read them that courage, faith, hope, joy, rose in my heart until I came to a place where I knew God would hear and answer this prayer. Then immediately I flipped the card over and read out my prayer to the Lord **and prayed it**, acting on **Mark 11:24**. Go to **Mark 11:24** and I will show you what I did. It says "**Therefore I say to you whatever things you ask when you pray…**"

Whatever things you ask…

I was going to ask for two houses to be sold on terms in ten days. Then my instruction from God was, "**believe that you receive them**." When am I supposed to believe that I received them? **At the time of prayer**, because that's what it said, "**When you pray**." Put a circle around **when** in your Bible, and write next to it the time you ask for it. I wrote on my card the exact time that I prayed that prayer, because at that exact time I had to do something. I had to believe that I received the answer to this prayer — that it is done from then on. I am not going to ask for it again, because if I believe I receive when I pray, why would I ask for it again, if I have already had it? Then I said, *"Thank you Father,"* because **Philippians 4:6** says, 'With thanksgiving make your requests known unto God.'"

I knelt at my bed, I raised my hands and I began to worship God. I said, *"Father I love you. I worship you. I love you Father. In the name of Jesus I worship you. I love you and I worship you. I love you Father and I worship you, I worship you, I worship you. Thank you for giving me the sale of two houses. Oh, I thank you Father. I worship you. I worship you. Thank you Father, thank you, thank you."* I did that for about seven minutes. I got up off my knees and I pointed to where I had been kneeling and said, *"Father, back there at such-and-such time I received two houses sold. I want to thank you for giving me that sale, seven minutes ago at that time. I want to thank you."* I stood there and worshipped Him a little more. Periodically through the day I did the same thing. Then, when I went to bed, I took my card out, read the scriptures, turned it over and read the prayer and just thanked God. I said, *"Father at this time I received that prayer answered. You gave me the sale of two houses, I have sold those two houses and I just want to thank you and worship you."*

The next morning I woke up, and before the devil could put any doubt in my head, I reached out just as I was coming to my senses, I grabbed that card, looked at those scriptures, read them out loud, turned it over, read the prayer and said, *"Father, yesterday at three o'clock Sunday afternoon*

I sold two houses and you did it for me and I just want to thank you," and I worshipped the Lord lying in the bed for a while.

Then I got up, had a shower, spent some time with the Lord, and went to work. Fodderings Hays and Hughes, the company I worked for in Durban North had an entrance hall area, and cubicles for the agents to sit in. There were about eight of us in that area. The partitioned dry wall was no higher than about five feet, so if you stood up you could see anybody else standing up in their cubicle. I came into the office and was on the look out for an estate agent I could talk to. I wanted to tell them I had sold two houses yesterday at three o'clock, because Jesus said in **Mark 11:23**, *"For assuredly, I say to you, whoever says to this mountain, 'Be removed and be cast into the sea,' and does not doubt in his heart, but believes that those things he says will be done, he will have whatever he says."* We need to say what we believe, that creates a higher level of faith in our own heart. I was trying to raise my level of faith, and not allow doubt to bombard my heart. So I planned to say my confession to the first person I saw.

While we are talking about this verse, let me mention a very helpful truth here, because the devil will always shoot arrows of doubt into your mind. The truth is you **can** doubt in your head and God **will** still answer your prayer, as long as you have faith in your heart. Because Jesus said, *"For assuredly I say to you whoever says to this mountain be removed and be cast into the sea and does not doubt **in his heart**."* He didn't say, 'Does not doubt in his head,' right? So, how do you know that you have faith in your heart, even though the devil is attacking you with doubt in your head? Jesus said, *"From the abundance of the heart the mouth speaks."* So listen to what a person says and that will tell you what's in his heart.

> You can doubt in your head and God will still answer your prayer, as long as you have faith in your heart.

As long as my words remain positive, *"I have sold two houses on terms,"* it doesn't matter what the devil says to me in my head, I can resist those doubtful thoughts and still stay in faith.

I walked up to the first estate agent, shook him by the hand and I said, *"Hey, guess what? I sold two houses Sunday afternoon at three o'clock on terms."*
He wasn't smiling. He wasn't happy. He didn't rejoice with me. He was upset. He looked bitter about it. He said, *"Well, where are those two houses?"*
I never expected to have to answer a question like that. Where are those two houses? I didn't have a clue where those two houses were. How would I know where they were? And I hadn't thought about what to say. That took me by surprise. I hadn't got my answer ready. I am trying to figure out what I am going to say because I do not want

to change my confession of faith. *"I've sold two houses on terms."* I said to him, *"I'm not going to tell you where they are. That's a secret."* I've used that line before. Remember? So he says, *"I need to know because I don't want to take clients there and waste their time, and mine. I want to remove those houses from the books."* Of course he's absolutely right. I didn't think about that. They're sold but I don't know which ones they are. So I just held fast to my confession and said, *"No, I'm not telling you."*

He said, *"Oh, okay."* He walked straight from there down the passage into Ed Waller's office, who was sitting behind his desk. Ed Waller was one of the directors. The agent walked in. I can't hear him but I can see what he's doing. I'm looking down this passage at Ed and I thought, *"All right, I'm going to get called in there in a minute, I guarantee that. What am I going say to the director? I cannot tell him where the houses are."* Ed Waller looks up at me, because obviously this guy is talking about me. Then he walked out, smiling, and said, *"Ed wants to see you."* (Now he is smiling, isn't that enough to make a monkey bite its mother?)

I walked in there and said, *"Hi Ed, you want to see me?"*

He said, *"Yes please, come sit down."* So I sat down. He said, *"Theo I believe you sold two houses yesterday."*

I said, *"Yes, on terms at three o'clock in the afternoon."*

"Oh, that's wonderful." He says, *"you know I need to take them out of the books because we can't have all the agents showing those houses when they are already sold. It is a waste of time."* He added, *"Would you kindly tell me where they are?"*

I said, *"Ed, with all respect to you I'm not going to tell you where they are. But I assure you of this Ed, very soon I will tell you, as soon as I have the freedom to tell you, I will tell you."*

Now he is frowning. I had been trying to teach him how faith works, and I had been asked how I sold so many houses. I was the top agent in the whole organization, selling four houses every month. Once I was asked to give them a big training course on how to sell houses. I took my Bible, took out **Mark 11:24** and started teaching them the word of God. I regret not giving an altar call, that's the only thing I regret.

Ed said, *"Theo, tell me. Did you really sell two houses on terms or is this one of them faith things?"*

I replied, *"Ed,* **Hebrews 11:1** *says 'faith is the evidence of things not seen.' Therefore whether I put a signed contract down on your desk, or walk in faith, there is no difference. It's a done deal. I have sold two houses on terms, I just wanted you to know."* So he looked at me, the frown is still on his face, he said, *"You know what? I will never understand you. You are dismissed."*

I thanked him and I walked out. Of course he can't understand me because reason and faith are completely different, two different worlds. That's why the Bible said, *"Trust* **in** *the Lord with all your heart and lean* **not** *to your own understanding."* Or you might say, 'have faith in God with all of your heart and do not depend only on reason.'

I proceeded to work from that moment. I'm desperate to find people to buy a house and take them out. If any person got into my car that I was going to show homes to, the first thing I did was tell them, *"Last Sunday at three o'clock in the afternoon I sold two houses on terms."* Could you imagine me getting into the car with a new client, and the first thing I want to do is make my confession to these complete strangers? I get into the car, close the door and say, *"Hi, let me tell you, last Sunday at three o'clock I sold two houses on terms."* And they just look at me with absolutely no expression on their face. I didn't care what they were thinking because I was a desperate man. My back was against the ropes. If they didn't buy any houses that day I'd bring them back to the office and as we were driving into the parking lot of Foddering Hays and Hughes, I'd say, *"Oh, by the way, did I mention to you that I sold two houses on terms last Sunday at three o'clock in the afternoon?"* They would look at me and some would say, *"Yes. You told me."* Others would just look, thank me for the ride and get out. They would look at each other like, *"What planet did this guy come from?"* I'd shake their hand and they would leave. I worked the whole week, and confessed it to all the agents, and to everybody I met. Twelve days went by. Now it is Thursday, and in 48 hours I have to pay the cash for the ring. I haven't sold any houses on terms in the natural. There hasn't been anybody even remotely interested in a house on terms. In fact not even one person asked about a house on terms. Anyhow, I'm confessing and praising God, worshipping the Lord all the time. *"Thank you Father."* Faith is more than a formula; it's more than a principle. It is a drawing closer to God in a relationship with your Heavenly Father. That's why I emphasize the worshipping of God in the process of believing for what you need. Worship God, not only when you're believing for something but every day. I encourage you when you're driving your car, worship God. Flying in a plane. When you are in the shower. Every spare moment you get, it should just come out of your mouth. If it's not coming out of you, start doing it, and make a habit of it. When you're lying in bed at night before you close your eyes think it, *"I love you, Father. I worship you. I love you. I worship you."*

Sometimes I wake up in the middle of the night, and lie there maybe for an hour and worship God. Bev's sleeping, my mouth's closed but I'm just worshipping God and telling Him that I love Him. The presence of God comes down in that bedroom so much that sometimes I lie there and weep. I want to encourage you to worship God and stay in the Spirit. There's no better way of drawing closer to God. The Bible said, *"Draw close to me and I'll draw close to you."* So draw close to Him by worshipping and He will draw close to you. You will sense His presence. If you're having a dry patch, just ask yourself how good your worship is. There's no such thing as a dry patch. It's a dry worship patch. It's a lack of worship, a lack of praise, a lack of giving credit where credit is due. It is a time of forgetting about God, that's why you sense the emptiness and the loneliness.

I took Arthur, a fellow agent and friend, out for a drive looking at homes this particular Thursday morning. When we got back to Foddering's, we sat in the car. He knew what was going on because he was a good friend. I had told him a couple of weeks earlier, *"Hey, you know Arthur, we're going to go choose a diamond ring and I don't have any money. Bev drew the ring she wants. Wow, it is expensive. I'm going to have to sell two houses on terms to get that amount of money, and I have to do it right away, I have to pray and ask God for this."* Arthur was concerned for me, because I put my credibility on the line. For the last few days I had not kept him up to speed with developments. Then he popped this question, *"Oh, by the way, you have about 48 hours before you have to pay the money, do you have it?"* The moment he said that, the reality hit me. The devil shot this huge arrow of doubt into my head. *"In 48 hours you have to have cash to pay for the ring."* Like arrows into my mind, the devil said, *"You haven't even got one enquiry for a house on terms."*

But this came out of my spirit. *"Praise God, Arthur, I have sold two houses on terms the previous Sunday at three o'clock in the afternoon. I have the money. I have no problem. Saturday I will go in there with the cash and pay for the ring."* When I said that to Arthur, I can't explain what happened to my heart. It was like God opened me up and just poured a swimming pool full of joy, peace and faith into my heart. The minute I said, *"I've got the money, I will pay cash on Saturday,"* it just overwhelmed me. I had so much joy, happiness and faith rush into my heart that I began to laugh. I sat in the car and laughed. Then I laughed longer and longer, one minute, two minutes, three minutes. I was aware of Arthur just sitting in the car next to me. He didn't get out. I thought, *"I'm glad I'm not God. God has a real problem. I believe I have sold two houses on terms. God has a real problem."* I knew I had it. I had done my part. I opened my eyes. I looked up at Arthur's face, he was looking down at me with an expression of pity and of concern. He was not smiling at all. Not even a hint of a smile. I could see it all over his face thinking, *"My friend's lost it. He is having a nervous breakdown. How am I going to help this poor man? He said he's going to pay for this ring, but he doesn't have the money. Now he is coming unglued."* Of course when I saw that, that didn't help me regain my composure. No, I just lost it completely at that point. I laughed so hard I almost had to be carried out of the car. For about 10 to 15 minutes I lay with my back on the seat and my knees on the steering wheel. Looking back, I realize that was the point the good fight of faith was won and Satan gave up.

The next day, Friday morning, I was sitting in the office, minding my own business. I heard the receptionist call out, *"There's a man out here who wants to buy a house and he's got no money."* If she had said there's a man out here, he's got 20, 50, 100,000 dollars and wants to buy a house, everyone would have stampeded to her. *"I'm too busy because this is such a waste of time,"* is how we treat folks who've got no money, and who want to buy a house. The Holy Spirit suddenly said, *"Okay, if he has no money, he will need to buy a house on terms, right?"* The Holy Spirit was explaining to me that this was the very man I was looking for. I jumped up and said at the top of my voice, *"I will take him out. I will take him out."* I ran down the passage in my excitement. You can imagine the look on this man's face, because he'd probably had very little interest shown to him at the other estate agents down the street. Now he was standing in Foddering Hays and Hughes and I ran down there, shouting at the top of my voice, *"I will take him out,"* with such excitement, while all our other agents are trying to act busy. He got in my car and first thing I said to him was, *"Hey, you know, two Sundays ago I sold two houses on terms."* We drove around, and looked at homes. Ninety percent of the owners were never home during the day since they were all at work. We walked into the third house and there was the owner of the home, a lady, sitting in her living room, coffee table in front of her and she was reading. With her permission, I showed the man the house. We went back to the car, and the man says, *"I want to buy that house."*

I said, *"Okay. Let's fill in the contract right now in the car."*

So he said, *"Okay, how much do you think she will come down to? What should I offer her?"*

I said, *"Now look, you want to buy on terms, right?"*

He said, *"Yeah."*

I said, *"You offer her the full price, because we've still got to get her to accept this whole concept of not getting her money for the sale of this home for the next five years. You are offering to rent it for five years while you save up a deposit to buy it. Only then does she get her money, in five years' time."*

"Okay," he agreed.

We filled in the contract, and we went back inside. I said to the lady, *"There are two things you need to know about this contract. Number one, it's a terms arrangement, which means they will rent it for five years and then the purchase comes into effect. During the five years they are going to save the money to put down a deposit. The second thing is that he's offering to purchase this home for full price, no discount offers."* I put this down on the table in front of her and she just stared at it for about three minutes. To me it seemed like three years. I did not say a word, because I could see her brain ticking over. She was probably rearranging her whole future. She was planning on getting her money **now**, and now she's thinking, *"Okay I have to rent something, I can't buy anything, I don't have cash from the sale of my home."* All sorts of things were probably going through her mind, and I can imagine that the Heavenly Father was helping her, through the Holy Spirit, to understand what action to take in this situation, so I sat there and watched as God did His work. Then she said, *"Where do I sign?"*

I said, *"Right here,"* and she signed that deal. I took the contract, went back to the car. I said to the purchaser, *"Now you need to write out a check for the first month's rental and the estate agent's commission and that'll be so much money."*

He said, *"Sure."* He wrote it out.

I asked, *"Is this check good?"*

He said, *"Yes."*

I went back to Foddering's, to receptionist, gave her the check and said, *"This check is good, it will not bounce. I'm saying it now, it will not bounce. You must bank it now, because Saturday morning I'm coming to pick up the money. I'd like you to have my commission in cash, ready to give to me."* It was about noon on Friday at this point.

At 1:30pm that Friday afternoon, I was sitting in my cubicle and I heard the receptionist say again, *"There's a man out here who wants to buy a house and he's got no money."*

I didn't need the Holy Spirit's help at that point. All by myself I figured out what I had to do. I just jumped up and shouted, *"I'll take him out."* I almost ran straight through that wall. I got down there and almost jumped into this man's arms. He stepped back and looked at me like, *"Wow, this guy's enthusiastic."*

We got in the car and I told him, *"Two Sundays ago I sold two houses on terms at three o'clock in the afternoon."* I then drove him around and showed him some houses. The third home we came to, you won't believe this, there was a man sitting in the house, just like the first situation. I showed the purchaser the house, took him back to the car and he said to me, *"I want to buy that house."*

We went through the same procedure. He said, *"What's the discount?"*

I said, *"No, you offer full price as you are purchasing on terms."* I filled in the contract, he signed it, and I went inside. I spoke to the seller, *"There's two things you have to know. **First**, it is a terms deal."* I explained what that meant. *"**Second**, there's no discount, he's offering you full price."* I put the offer down on the table in his living room. He stared at this contract for about three minutes. Once again, it seemed like three years. He and I never said a word. I guess the same thing went through his mind as with the lady earlier on. Then finally, he said, *"Where do I sign?"* He signed it and I thought to myself, *"I cannot believe I am reliving the exact same expe-*

rience I had a few hours ago." I went to the car, the purchaser wrote up the check for the estate agent's commission and the first month's rental. I gave it to the receptionist and I said, *"Please go to the bank right away and deposit this before the bank closes today. It is good, it will not bounce. I need my commission paid out in cash tomorrow morning. I will be here to pick up the cash from both sales."*

The next morning I came to the office. Both checks were good, I got my cash, put it in my pocket, went round to Bev's, picked her up, and we drove to the jewelry store. She asked, *"Do you have the money?"* I said, *"Of course I have the money. What do you think? Of course I have the money. Sure I have the money."* We picked up the ring. She loved it. I kept it since I was going to put it on her finger that night. I dropped her off and then I went over to Fred Robert's house, he was the Pastor of the church, where I had been attending for only a few months. I said, *"Pastor Fred, there's no way I'm going to keep this money until Sunday. I want you to take it now. It's burning a hole in my pocket."* And I gave him the 20% tithe. I said, *"Please put this in the church offering for me tomorrow."*

He said, *"Fine."* He didn't understand what that was all about but he took it. That night I took Bev out to the best restaurant in Durban, and it cost quite a bit of money but it was worth every cent. I placed the ring on her finger and we got engaged. After I dropped her off that night, and I was driving home I wondered how much money I had left. I put my hands in my pockets and turned them inside out, I found a five-cent coin. I put it on the dashboard next to my steering wheel and I looked at that coin as I drove home. I thought about all I had been through the last fourteen days since I stood in that jewelry store. I wondered to myself why I did not ask for a little extra to at least get me some gas (petrol) money and food for the next few days!

Because I believed God he arranged two purchasers to come in on Friday, the day before I had to pay the money over. He arranged two purchases. He ordered the steps of those two buyers to come to Fodderings. They had no idea they were being sent there by the angels. The other agents sat still and they had no idea that they were being kept in their seats. Then the two sellers of their homes had no idea why they weren't at work or whatever they were supposed to be that day, but they were both at home waiting for me. If either one of those sellers had been working like everyone normally was, I would have had to go out on Friday night and see them when they came home from work. The banks would have been closed and I wouldn't have gotten my cash until Monday. The Heavenly Father arranged the actions of several people just to make this happen for me. Why did it happen at the last moment? I don't know. Did it take time for the angels to put all those things in line? I don't know. I received what I asked for at the time I prayed, and held onto my confession of faith. I believed it **was** done and God did it — that's good enough for me. All I know is, that Jesus said it, I believed it, and it worked.

Say this, *"When you believe God, whoever God needs to organize He will do it. If I believe God, whatever circumstances He needs to arrange for me, He'll do it."*

Say this, *"The word of God is true. I can depend on every word in the Bible. I can act on it. God always answers prayer. He is a God who answers prayer. Whatever I need, He will give me, if I dare to believe."*

God delights in His children believing Him for things, for salvations, for everything, for anything. God the Father wants us to have an ongoing faith relationship with Himself, drawing closer to Him, getting answers from Him, getting excited about prayer.

> The word of God is true. I can depend on every
> word in the Bible. I can act on it. God always
> answers prayer. He is a God who answers prayer.
> Whatever I need, He will give me, if I dare to
> believe.

Chapter Thirteen

Deliberately Bringing God's Plans and Blessings Into Our World, By Speaking Positive Words.

> **Matthew 17:1 (NKJ)** *Now after six days Jesus took Peter, James, and John his brother, led them up on a high mountain by themselves;*
>
> *² and He was **transfigured** before them. His face shone like the sun, and His clothes became as white as the light.*
>
> *³ And behold, Moses and Elijah appeared to them, talking with Him.*
>
> *⁴ Then Peter answered and said to Jesus, "Lord, it is good for us to be here; if You wish, let us make here three tabernacles: one for You, one for Moses, and one for Elijah."*
>
> *⁵ While he was still speaking, behold, a bright cloud overshadowed them; and suddenly a voice came out of the cloud, saying, "This is My beloved Son, in whom I am well pleased. Hear Him!"*
>
> *⁶ And when the disciples heard it, they fell on their faces and were greatly afraid.*

Notice the word, '**transfigured**' in Matthew 17 verse 2. This is No. 3339 in the Strong's Hebrew/Greek/English dictionary. It is the Greek word, '**Mĕtamŏrphŏō**'. The English word is '**metamorphosis**', which means, *"to change, to transfigure, to transform"*. As we know the original New Testament was written in Greek. **The original Greek word used to describe what happened to Jesus** when **His face began to shine like the sun**, and **His clothes became white as light**, because the glory of God in Him could not be contained, **is this word 'metamorphosis'**. This is the same word we use to describe what happens to a caterpillar when it becomes a butterfly.

Now look at **Romans 12:1-2:**

> **Romans 12:1 (NKJ)** *I beseech you therefore, brethren, by the mercies of God, that you present your bodies a living sacrifice, holy, acceptable to God, which is your reasonable service.*
>
> *² And do not be conformed to this world, **but be transformed by the renewing of your mind**, that you may prove what is that good and acceptable and perfect will of God.*

Notice the word of God tells us to be **transformed** by the renewing of our mind. What does this mean? It means that, **as we meditate in the word of God, we are transformed into what we see in the Word, we become like Christ. The glory of Christ becomes visible through our lives**. We begin walking in the good and perfect will of God for our lives.

The word '**transformed**' here in **Romans 12:2**, is the same Greek word, No. 3339, used to describe what happened to Jesus in **Matthew 17** when He was **transfigured_(transformed)**. The glory of God began to shine through Jesus. **Romans 12:2** is telling us we can have the same experience that Jesus had, by allowing the word of God to saturate our heart and mind.

We can be changed into the image of Christ - the life of Christ can be fully manifest through our lives - His nature, character, love, power, anointing. **That's who the new creation man is. It's Christ Himself living through us. That's what God paid for at Calvary**.

> *2 Corinthians 3:18 (AMP) And all of us, as with unveiled face, [because we] continued to behold [in the Word of God] as in a mirror the glory of the Lord, (we) are constantly being **transfigured into His very own image** in ever increasing splendor and **from one degree of glory to another**; [for this comes] from the Lord [Who is] the Spirit.*

Transfigured — there is that Greek word again, Mĕtamŏrphŏō, which in English is **Metamorphosis**. **2 Corinthians 3:18** is telling us that as we read the word of God, we see what God says about us. It's like we are looking into a mirror, we see ourselves. **We see who we really are as a new creation in Christ**. Much like a kitten looking into a mirror and seeing a huge male lion looking back at him out of the mirror. As the kitten continues looking into the mirror and seeing itself as a lion, it begins to change into the lion it sees. **As we continue to look into the Word we see ourselves as God sees us, the new creation**.

We are changed into the very image of Christ, from one degree of glory to another, in ever-increasing splendor. **We become what we really are, what God has created us to be in Christ**.

> In **John 6:63**, Jesus said, "**It is the (Holy) Spirit who gives Life...the words that I speak to you are (Holy) Spirit, and they are Life**."

As we look into the scriptures, the life of Christ fills our being with His nature, His character, His attributes, His abilities...

Step one is to understand the power of positive words. We need a God-given revelation of the subject. Once we understand the many benefits of speaking positive words, we need to put it into practice.

Therefore **step number two** would be to deliberately begin speaking positively into the various dimensions of our life. For example, spiritual, mental, physical, family, financial, etc.

Let's begin by declaring over ourselves, what God says about us.

Now let's look at God's image of us!

236

In other words, let's read, declare, and meditate on scriptures that describe who we are as the new creation.

> **Ephesians 2:8 (NLT)** *God saved you by His special favor **when you believed**. And you can't take credit for this; it is a gift from God.*
>
> *⁹ Salvation is not a reward for the good things we have done, so none of us can boast about it.*

Boldly declare — *"The Heavenly Father has received me as His beloved child; I am bound for heaven, all because I believe in Jesus and declare Him to be the Lord of my life."*

> **Romans 8:16 (NKJ)** *The Holy Spirit Himself bears witness with our spirit that **we are children of God**,*
>
> *¹⁷ and if children, then heirs, **heirs of God and joint heirs with Christ.***

Boldly declare — *"I am God's very own child, I have inherited all that belongs to my Father, and I am an equal heir of all that belongs to Jesus Christ my Lord."*

*"It's not only what Christ owns that I have inherited - **I have also inherited who Christ is. He Himself is alive in me - living through me. We have become one life**. This is what I have inherited."*

> **Romans 8:15 (NLT)** *So **you should not be like cowering, fearful slaves**. You should*

behave instead like God's very own children,
*adopted into his family - calling him "Father, dear
Father."*

¹⁶ *For his Holy Spirit speaks to us deep in our hearts
and tells us that **we are God's children***.

Boldly declare — *"I am no longer a slave of sickness, lack,
fear, circumstances, or the devil. I am God's very own child, and
I behave like I am."*

¹⁷ *And **since we are his children, we will share
his treasures - <u>for everything God gives to
his Son, Christ, is ours, too</u>**. But if we are to
share his glory, we must also share his suffering (the
suffering here refers to us making sacrifices to spread
the gospel of salvation).*

Boldly declare — *"Everything the Father has given to Christ,
He has given to me. **<u>I am a covenant partner of all Christ
has received</u>**."*

Boldly declare — *"**<u>What God did for Christ at the resurrection, He was doing for me</u>. Christ was my substitute**."*

God paid for me to have:
- All the **attributes** of Christ.
- All the **qualities** of Christ.
- All the **abilities** of Christ.
- The **nature** and **character** of Christ.
- I am **wise** with Christ's wisdom.

- I am **strong** with Christ's strength.
- I am **righteous** with Christ's righteousness.
- I am **alive** with the life of Christ.
- I am **complete** in Christ.

> **Ephesians 4:24 (NLT)** *You **must display** a new nature because **you are a new person**, **created in God's likeness** - righteous, holy, and true.*

Boldly declare — *"I am born again into the very likeness of God. **Whatever God the Father did to Christ in His death burial and resurrection, He was doing to me as part of the new creation.**"*

> **Colossians 3:3a (NLT)** *For you died when Christ died...*

> **2 Corinthians 5:14b (NKJ)** *...if One died for all, then all died.*

Boldly declare — *"When Christ died on the cross, I was being crucified for my sins in Christ."*

> **Romans 6:4a (NKJ)** *Therefore we were buried with Him...*
>
> *⁵ For if we have been united together in the likeness of His death...*

239

Boldly declare — *"When Christ was buried in the tomb, I was buried in that tomb, in Christ."*

> **Ephesians 2:4 (NKJ)** *But God, who is rich in mercy, because of His great love with which He loved us,*
>
> *⁵ even when we were dead in trespasses, **made us alive together with Christ**...*

Boldly declare — *"When Christ was raised from the dead, on the third day by the glory of the Father, I was raised from the dead by the glory of the Father in Christ."*

> **Ephesians 2:6a (NKJ)** *and raised us up together...*

Boldly declare — *"When Christ ascended toward heaven, I ascended to heaven in Christ."*

> **Ephesians 2:6b (NKJ)** *...and made us sit together in the heavenly places in Christ Jesus*

Boldly declare — *"When Christ sat down triumphantly as a conqueror, on the right hand of the Father in heaven, I sat down as a conqueror on the right hand of the Father in Christ."*

> **Ephesians 2:10a (NKJ)** *For we are His (God's) workmanship, created **in** Christ Jesus...*

Boldly declare — *"When God was raising Christ in the resurrection, He was creating the new creation. God was bringing forth a new species of being into the earth. What God was doing to Christ in the resurrection, He was doing to the new creation man, because **we,** <u>the new creation, and **Christ** are **one**</u> <u>in Christ</u>. I am His workmanship."*

> **Ephesians 5:30 (NKJ)** *For we are members of His body, of His flesh and of His bones.*

Boldly declare — *"I am one with Christ, I am part of His flesh, His body and His bones."*

> **1 Corinthians 6:17 (NKJ)** *But he who is joined to the Lord is **one spirit** with Him.*

Boldly declare — *"I am the spirit of Christ, and the spirit of Christ is me, **<u>we are one spirit together in Christ</u>.**"*

> **Ephesians 2:6b (NLT)** *...all because **we are one with Christ Jesus.***

Boldly declare — *"This is how God sees me, **this is what God paid for me to be at the resurrection**. Yes, I am God's workmanship, He personally created me this way in Christ Jesus."*

> **Romans 8:29a (NKJ)** *...God also predestined (us) to be conformed to the image of His Son...*

This scripture refers to our conduct.

Boldly declare — *"God is keeping me holy, spirit, soul and body. I am behaving more like Christ every day."*

> ***1 John 4:17b (NKJ)*** …**As Christ is, so are we in this world**.

This scripture refers to our legal inheritance of all Christ is.

Boldly declare — *"The Heavenly Father sees me with all that Christ is, has, and can do, because that is how He made me in Christ. That's what He paid for through Christ.* **As I meditate on these scriptures and declare them, I am changed into this glorious splendor from one degree of glory to another**. *Christ Himself is risen in me. It is no longer I that liveth, Christ is alive in me."*

> ***Ephesians 1:21 (NLT)*** *Now* **Christ is far above any ruler or authority or power or leader or anything else in this world or in the world to come.**

The Father has placed Christ as the commander of this universe, and all future universes to come. All things must obey Christ when commanded to.

> ***Ephesians 1:22 (NLT)*** *And* **God has put all things under the authority of Christ,** *and* **God gave Christ this authority for the benefit of the church**.

Boldly declare — *"<u>**God gave Christ this authority for my**</u> <u>**benefit**</u>. With Christ's authority I command circumstances to line up with the will of God. Just like Jesus spoke to the storm on the Sea of Galilee when He was in the boat,* **I speak to the storms of life <u>with that same authority</u>, the authority of Christ, and <u>the storms of life still obey that authority</u> <u>today</u>**.*"

> **Ephesians 2:6 (NLT)** *For God raised us from the dead along with Christ, and we are seated with him in the heavenly realms —* **all because we are <u>one</u> with Christ Jesus***.*

Boldly declare — *"I am seated with Christ on the right hand of the Father in the throne room.* **<u>I am seated in the finished</u> <u>work of Calvary. I rest in the victory Christ won</u>, and conquered for me through Calvary**.*"

> **Romans 8:37 (NKJ)** *Yet in all these things we are more than conquerors* **through Him** *who loved us.*

Boldly declare — *"Yet* **in** *all these things,* **in** *the heat of the battle, I am more than a conqueror through Him who loved me, because victory for every battle in my future has already been paid for in Christ."*

> **Philippians 4:13** *"I can do all things through Christ who strengthens me."*

Boldly declare — *"The supernatural ability of Christ enables me to carry out my everyday duties and responsibilities. The supernatural ability of Christ enables me to accomplish impossible tasks, and do great exploits that God has planned for my life, to advance the kingdom of Christ in the earth."*

> **1 John 3:1 (NKJ)** Behold **what manner of love the Father has bestowed on us, that we should be called children of God**!
>
> ^{2a} Beloved, now we **are** children of God…

Boldly declare — *"The Heavenly Father loves me as His own personal beloved child."*

> **1 Corinthians 1:30 (NKJ)** But of God you are **in Christ** Jesus, who became for us **wisdom** from God, and **righteousness**, and **sanctification** and **redemption**,

Boldly declare — *"I am wise with Christ's wisdom. I am righteous with Christ's righteousness.*

Christ is my sanctifier
Christ is my redeemer.
Christ is my widsom.
Christ is my righteousness."

> **Colossians 3:4 (NKJ)** When **Christ** who **is our life** appears, then you also will appear with Him in glory.

Boldly declare — *"I am alive with the life of Christ."*

> **Colossians 2:10 (NKJ)** <u>and you are complete in Christ</u>...

Boldly declare — *"I am complete in Christ. I have inherited all Christ owns. I have inherited all Christ can do. **<u>I have inherited all that Christ is</u>**. I am complete in Christ. I am completely healthy, prosperous, wise, successful, fulfilled, and productive in God's Kingdom. Christ purchased all this for me, **<u>I am complete in Him</u>**."*

> **2 Corinthians 5:17 (NKJ)** *Therefore, if anyone is in Christ, **he is a new creation**; old things have passed away; **behold, all things have become new**.*

Boldly declare — *"Because I am in Christ, I am a new creation, I am a new species of being, **<u>I am created in the image of Christ</u>**."*

> **John 15:5a (NKJ)** *The Lord Jesus said -* "**I am the vine, you are the branches**. *He who abides in Me, and I in him, bears much fruit; for without Me you can do nothing."*
>
> [7] **If you abide in Me, and My words abide in you**, *you will ask what you desire, and it shall be done for you.*

245

Jesus is the vine which is the trunk or the stem and we are the branch attached to Jesus. Notice the **branch** and the **stem** (the **trunk**), (the **vine**) are all part of **one tree**.

Boldly declare — *"The life of the **root** and the **trunk** flows into the **branches**. I am a branch, I am joined to Christ, His life is flowing into me, as I abide in His Word. The life that keeps Christ alive keeps me alive, the life of Christ."*

Boldly declare — *"The life that is in the root, in Christ, is in me. The nature that is in the root, in Christ, is in me. The power that is in the root, in Christ, is in me."*

"<u>As I continue to meditate in these truths, this will become evident in my life</u>."

Boldly declare — *"What Jesus did for the people, I must do for the people in His place. I am His representative in the earth today. I must calm the storms of life in His place, **<u>with His authority</u>**."*

> **2 Corinthians 5:21** *For the Father made Christ who never sinned to be sin for us, that we might become the righteousness of God **in Him**.*

Righteousness means right standing with God. This does not mean that you are living a perfect life. It simply means that God has declared you **innocent** in His eyes. You have right standing in His eyes. Jesus Christ who is righteous before God, has become your righteousness in your place.

Boldly declare — *"I am righteous in the eyes of God, I am completely innocent. Christ is my righteousness."*

> **Romans 8:1 (NLT)** *So now there is no condemnation for those who belong to Christ Jesus.*

Boldly declare — *"I stand in the presence of God without the sense of sin, without the sense of guilt, without the sense of shame, such is the degree, the quality, the perfection of my redemption."*

> **John 5:24 (NLT)** *"I assure you, those who listen to my message and believe in God who sent me have eternal life. They will never be condemned for their sins, but **they have already passed from death into life**."*

Boldly declare — *"**I have already passed from death into eternal life. I will never be condemned for my sin**. If I make a mistake, I can ask the Father to forgive me, and He does, according to **1 John 1:9**."*

> **1 John 1:9 (NLT)** *But if **we** (we includes John the Apostle) confess **our** sins (our includes John the Apostle) to God, He is faithful and just to forgive **us** (us includes John the Apostle) and to cleanse **us** (us includes John the Apostle) from **every** wrong.*

Boldly declare — *"If I, as a Christian, am sorry for a sin I commit, and ask the Father to forgive me for it, He is faithful* *and just, He will surely forgive me, and cleanse me from every wrong. **<u>This is what the Apostle John did when he made a mistake. If it worked for John, it works for me</u>**.*"

Please remember, **sanctification** is another word for **holiness**. Christ is ensuring that we grow in holiness. He is seeing to it that we become more set apart (sanctified) for His purpose every day.

Righteousness and **holiness** are not the same thing. Righteousness means that God has declared you innocent of all sin. You have right standing with God. **Holiness** refers to your **conduct** and **behavior**. To the degree that you are obedient to God, that will determine the degree of your holiness. **Holiness** simply means I am **available** to God anywhere, anytime for any purpose. I am being **led by the Spirit of God**, I don't live for myself. We are all at different levels of holiness. We have all achieved a level of holiness and we are still growing further in holiness. Holiness is not only **abstaining** from what is wrong, it is also being **available** to do what is right, what God asks us to do.

<u>Like a glove on your hand</u>. The glove is holy to your hand. It only does what the hand wants to do through it. It never works independently of the hand. That's holiness.

<u>Like a paintbrush in the hand of the Master painter</u>. It will never work independently of the hand, neither will it take the glory and the honor for the painting. That's holiness.

> **Hebrews 10:14 (NLT)** *For by that one offering he perfected forever (declared righteous) all those whom he is **making holy**.*

Boldly declare — *"Even though the Heavenly Father sees me innocent and righteous in His eyes, I am growing in my conduct, and in my holiness."*

> **Hebrews 2:11 (NKJ)** *For both Christ who sanctifies and those who are **being sanctified** are all of **one**, for which reason He is not ashamed to call them brethren.*

Boldly declare — *"According to **Hebrews 2:11**, Christ is sanctifying my life, making me holy, my conduct is improving every day."*

> **2 Corinthians 1:21 (NIV)** *Now it is God who **makes** both us and you **stand firm** in Christ.*

Boldly declare — *"Father, thank you for making me **stand firm** in Christ. Thank you for **keeping me holy**. Thank you for **keeping me faithful**. Thank you for **keeping me in your perfect will**. Thank you for **keeping my thoughts pure**. Thank you for **keeping my heart motives pure**. My faith is in you to keep me. I do **not** trust in my own strength."*

> **2 Corinthians 1:22 (NIV)** *(God has) **set his seal of ownership on us**, and **put his Spirit in***

> **our hearts as a deposit**, **guaranteeing** *what is*
> *to come.*

Boldly declare – *"The born-again experience of the indwelling Holy Spirit is the guarantee of my salvation. This is God's seal of ownership on my life."*

Boldly declare — *"Just as a king would put the seal of his ring on something in the store, declaring, 'this is mine,' and the store owner would deliver it immediately, even so, the Father has put His seal on my life. Satan knows I am God's property."*

> **Ephesians 4:30 (NKJ)** *And do not grieve the Holy Spirit of God, by whom you were* **sealed** *for the day of redemption.*

Boldly declare — *"I declare the indwelling Holy Spirit is the seal that guarantees that I will be taken up in the Rapture when Jesus returns. The indwelling Holy Spirit, of the born-again experience, is my guarantee that God has purchased me, and that I am His beloved child. I am sealed."*

Boldly declare — *"Unless I deliberately choose to **walk away from Christ**, and choose to live in the world **without Christ**, I will most definitely go to heaven. **I am sealed**. All this is mine because I am **in Christ**."*

Boldly declare — *"I will hear, 'Well done good and faithful servant, enter thou into the joy of your Lord,' because my faith is in Christ to accomplish this in my life. I am not depending on the flesh."*

> **Romans 5:17b (NKJ)** . . . *those who* **receive**
> *abundance of grace and of the* **gift** *of righteousness*
> *will reign in life* **through the One, Jesus Christ**.

Boldly declare — *"Because of the grace of God, I can exercise the authority of Christ to reign as a king in this life."*

> **Ephesians 1:22 (NLT)** *And God has put* **all**
> **things under the authority of Christ**, *and God*
> *gave Christ this authority* <u>**for the benefit of the**</u>
> <u>**church**</u>.

Boldly declare — *"Christ was given this authority for my benefit."*

> **Matthew 28:18 (NKJ)** *And Jesus came and spoke*
> *to them, saying,* "<u>**All authority**</u> *has been given to*
> *Me in heaven and on earth.*
> [19] **Go therefore** *and make disciples of all the*
> *nations, baptizing them in the name of the Father*
> *and of the Son and of the Holy Spirit,*

Boldly declare — *"It is the will of Christ that I go in His authority and bring His love to this lost world. I command circumstances to line up with the will of God."*

> **Luke 10:19 (NKJ)** *Behold,* <u>**I give you the**</u>
> <u>**authority**</u> *to trample on serpents and scorpions,*
> <u>**and over all the power of the enemy**</u>, *and*
> *nothing shall by any means hurt you.*

Boldly declare — "<u>**The authority of Christ has been given to me to use in this world, as I represent Christ**</u>. *Therefore I will walk on Satan and demons, not with my feet but with the words of my mouth. He will not stop me,* <u>**nothing will stop God's word from working for me**</u>."

> **Colossians 1:13 (NKJ)** *The heavenly Father* **has delivered us from the power of darkness** *and conveyed us into the kingdom of the Son of His love,*
>
> [14] **in Christ** *we have redemption through His blood, the forgiveness of sins.*

Boldly declare — *"This is not something I am trying to get –* <u>**I have already been delivered from the authority of darkness**</u>. *I have already been transferred into the kingdom of Christ. Satan is no match for me, no matter* **where** *I meet him, no matter* **what** *the test.* **Satan's dominion over me has ended** *– and the* **dominion of the Lord Jesus over me began** *– the moment I declared Jesus to be my new Lord and Savior."*

Boldly declare — *"Just like Israel was free forever from the Pharaoh, after his army drowned in the Red Sea, so I am free forever from Satan after Jesus conquered him through His death, burial and resurrection."*

"**I have now become Satan's master through Calvary.** <u>**That is who the new creation is**</u>**, that is what God paid for, that's who I am through Christ**."

Ephesians 1:7 (NKJ) In Christ *we have redemption through His blood, the forgiveness of sins, __according to the riches of His grace__.*

Boldly declare — *"Because I am in Christ, God has forgiven me and He is pouring out the riches of His glorious blessings into my life."*

The Lord Jesus said in:

John 6:63 (NKJ) It is the (Holy) Spirit who gives Life…__the words that I speak to you are (Holy) Spirit and they are Life__.

Matthew 8:16 (NKJ) *When evening had come, they brought to Him many who were demon-possessed. And He cast out the spirits with a word,* **and healed all who were sick,**

[17] that it might be fulfilled which was spoken by Isaiah the prophet, saying: **"He Himself took our infirmities and bore our sicknesses**.*"*

Isaiah 53:4 *Surely Jesus Christ* **has borne our sicknesses and carried our pains**…

*[5] …***by whose wounds we are healed**.

1 Peter 2:24b (NKJ) *… by* **whose** *stripes you* **were** *healed.*

Boldly declare — *"The Lord Jesus suffered with my pains, He suffered with my sicknesses, so I don't have to bear them. The wounds He bore purchased my healing. My body is well. These words are Holy Spirit and they are Life. As I meditate on these words, the life and health and healing of Christ continually flows through my body."*

> **Psalm 27:1 (NKJ)** . . . *the Lord is the strength of my life.*

> **Psalm 107:20 (NKJ)** *God sent His* **word** *and healed them — and delivered them from their destructions.*

Boldly declare — *"The Lord is the strength of my life, His strength fills my body.* **God sent His Word to bring health to me***. I declare His health and strength is flowing through my body. Praise God, I love you Jesus."*

Boldly declare — *"When God raised Christ completely* **well** *and* **whole** *from the dead, I* **was** *raised completely* **well** *and* **whole** *at the same time. This is how God sees the new creation,* **and this is how God sees me***. This is what God paid for."*

> **Romans 8:2 (NKJ)** *For the law of the Spirit of life in Christ Jesus has made me free from the law of sin and death.*

What is the **law** of the **spirit of life** in Christ Jesus? The **law** of the **spirit of life** in Christ Jesus is the **salvation** that the

Lord Jesus **freely** gave us, through His death and resurrection. This law has made me free from another law, **the law of sin and death**. According to the Old Testament law, sin would result in death. This is confirmed in the New Testament.

> **Romans 6:23a (NKJ)** *For the wages of sin is death...*

Because we have received Christ into our hearts, and been placed by the Father into Christ, we are a **new creation**, **a new species of being**. All those **new** creation people who are **in Christ** will **not** experience death as a result of their **past** sin, because the new **law** of the **spirit of life in Christ Jesus** has set us free from the **law of sin and death**.

Boldly declare — *"The **salvation** given through Christ has **set me free** from the **death** I should have received because I broke the law."*

> **Romans 8:11** *But if the (Holy) Spirit of the Father who raised Jesus from the dead dwells in you, the Father who raised Christ from the dead will also give life to your mortal bodies through the (Holy) Spirit who dwells in you.*

Boldly declare — *"Thank you Father for the life of the Holy Spirit that is flowing through my body. His **healing** is flowing through me now, His **health** is flowing through me now, His **strength** is flowing through me now, His **youth** is flowing* *through me now, His **vitality** is flowing through me now, His* **encouragement** *is flowing through me now.* **I see myself well**, *enjoying life to the full. Witnessing for Christ freely."*

> **Revelation 5:10 (NKJ)** *(Jesus Christ) has made us kings and priests to our God; and we shall reign on the earth.*

Your priestly ministry is your ministry to God. Your **kingly** ministry **is your ministry on behalf of God to this world.**

> **Romans 5:17b (NKJ)** . . . *much more **those who receive** abundance of **grace** and of the **gift** of righteousness **will reign in life** through the One, (Jesus Christ.)*

Boldly declare — *"I accept all that God has done for me as a new creation, by His grace. I will reign like a king in this life, because that is who I am. This is what God paid for, and I will appropriate it."*

Even if you have $1,000 in your pocket you can die from starvation if you don't spend it. **Let us use the authority that is ours**, the **wisdom** that is ours, the **favor** and the **blessing** that is ours. Let us be bold to declare who we are as a new creation in Christ, and what He will do through us in this world.

> **John 14:12 (NKJ)** *"Most assuredly, I say to you, he who believes in Me, the **works** that I do he will*

> do also; and greater **works** than these he will do,
> because I go to My Father.
>
> [13] And whatever you ask **(<u>command</u>**, in the Greek)
> in My name, that I will do, that the Father may be
> glorified in the Son.
>
> 14 If you ask **(<u>command</u>)** anything in My name, I
> will do it."

The root Greek word for "**ask**" is "**command**". We are **not** commanding God to do anything; we **are** commanding the **circumstances** of life to line up with God's will, on behalf of God.

Just like Peter at The Gate Beautiful in **Acts 3**, he commanded the lame man to be healed on behalf of Jesus. Peter did not stop and pray to God the Father, he never asked God to do this miracle. Jesus said **we will do the same works** He did. We **must** command His works to manifest in Jesus' name. **Only** when we command does God act in response to our words. If God was going to change this world on His own without us, it would have been changed by now. **God is waiting for us to speak to the circumstances of life**.

> **Matthew 18:18 (NKJ)** Assuredly, I say to you,
> whatever **you** bind on earth will be bound in heaven,
> and whatever **you** loose on earth will be loosed in
> heaven.

This is exactly how a **king reigns** over His Kingdom; **He makes decrees by speaking** them forth. The king's words are final authority. We must understand when we speak the words of **King Jesus**, they are **final authority** in the earth, circumstances **must** come in line with His words coming out of our mouths.

Boldly declare — *"I speak as a king in the earth, **in the realm of the spirit, I take Christ's place <u>with His author-ity</u>**. I command circumstances to line up with the will of God in Jesus' name."*

> **Hebrews 1:13 (NKJ)** *But to which of the angels has He ever said: "Sit at My right hand, till I make Your enemies Your footstool?"*
> *14 Are they not all ministering spirits sent forth to minister **for those who will inherit salvation?***

Most people read that as the angels are sent forth to minister **to** those who will inherit salvation. Changing the word from *"**for**"* to the word *"**to**"* makes a world of difference to that statement.

> **Hebrews 1:14 (NKJ)** *Are they not all ministering spirits sent forth to minister **for those who will inherit salvation?***

Angels are waiting for our instructions, <u>**just like a waiter in a restaurant**</u>.

> **Numbers 6:22 (NKJ)** *And the Lord spoke to*
> *Moses, saying:*
>
> [23] *Speak to Aaron and his sons, saying, 'This is the*
> *way you shall bless the children of Israel.'* **Say to**
> **them***:*
>
> [24] *The Lord bless you and keep you;*
>
> [25] *The Lord make His face shine upon you, and be*
> *gracious to you;*
>
> [26] *The Lord lift up His countenance upon you, and*
> *give you peace.*
>
> [27] **"So they shall put My name on the**
> **children of Israel, and I will bless them***."*

In other words God is saying, "**I need you to speak a**
blessing <u>so that</u> I can bring the blessing to pass. I want
to bring my blessings into the earth but I need you to
speak it **so I can do it**. Remember, whatever you **forbid**
and whatever you **allow**, heaven will agree with according
to **Matthew 18:18**.

> **Numbers 14:28 (NKJ)** *(Moses), say to the*
> *children of Israel,* **'As I live,'** *says the Lord,* **'just**
> **as you have spoken in My hearing, <u>so I will</u>**
> **<u>do to you</u>***.*

Those who say they can't and those who say they can, are
both right. God says you will get what you say.

> **Philippians 4:19 (NKJ)** *And my God shall supply all your need according to His riches in glory* **by Christ Jesus**.

Boldly declare — *"Because I am in Christ, God has guaranteed to supply all my need according to His riches in glory."*

Boldly declare — *"I am not limited to earth's economy.* ***Nothing*** *can stop* ***God's Word*** *from working in my life.* ***God's financial provision*** *belongs to me* ***because*** *I am a new creation."*

Boldly declare — *"Finances are flowing into my life from every direction.* ***Angels of God, you are released*** *to bring the money to me.* ***Satan and demon spirits, you are bound,*** *you cannot stop my harvest from coming to me."*

Boldly declare — *"I have given, therefore it is given back to me, good measure, pressed down, shaken together and running over. Everybody wants to do business with me. I have God's wisdom to create financial increase. I am a fundraiser for the gospel. Because I am a tither, I am receiving ideas from the Holy Spirit, to earn extra money."*

> **Ephesians 1:3 (NLT)** *How we praise God, the Father of our Lord Jesus Christ, who* **has blessed** *us with* **every** *spiritual* **blessing** *in the heavenly realms* **because we belong to Christ**.

Boldly declare — *"Every blessing that God has belongs to me. Therefore I declare that I am already blessed, with every blessing, that is what belongs to the new creation."*

> **Romans 8:32 (NLT)** Since **God did not spare even his own Son** *but gave him up for us all - won't God - who gave us Christ -* **also give us everything else?**

Boldly declare — *"All things are mine because I am a new creation."*

> **1 Corinthians 1:5 (NIV)** *In Christ* **you have been enriched in every way** *– in all your speaking and all your knowledge.*

Boldly declare — *"I am enriched in every way, because I am in Christ."*

> **1 Corinthians 15:57 (AMP)** *But thanks be to God -* **Who gives us the victory** *[making us conquerors] through our Lord Jesus Christ.*

Boldly declare — *"**Because I am in Christ, God has guaranteed victory in every situation of life going forward.** Because I am in Christ**, I have already conquered every challenge I will ever face in my future."*

> **2 Corinthians 2:14 (NIV)** *But thanks be to God, **who always leads us** in triumphal procession in Christ . . .*

Boldly declare — *"Because I am a new creation in Christ, God has guaranteed to lead me throughout this life, in triumphal procession. Praise God He's leading me from one victory to another."*

> **Philippians 3:13 (NLT)** *No, dear brothers and sisters, I am still not all I should be, but I am focusing all my energies on this one thing: **Forgetting the past** and **looking forward to what lies ahead**,* [14] *I strain to reach the end of **the race** and receive **the prize** for which God, through Christ Jesus, is calling us up to heaven.*

Boldly declare — *"I am not going to allow my past mistakes to stop me. I am running God's race. **I am looking forward to the prize Jesus will give me when I get to heaven**."*

> **Colossians 1:28 (NKJ)** *Christ we preach, warning every man and teaching every man in all wisdom, that we may present every man perfect (Christian maturity) in Christ Jesus.*

> **Colossians 1:29 (NLT)** *I work very hard at this, as **I depend** on Christ's **mighty power** that works within me.*

Boldly declare — *"I am working with God's mighty power flowing through me, to extend His kingdom in this earth. I am fulfilling God's plan and purpose for my life. He is ordering my steps."*

> **2 Timothy 1:9 (NKJ)** *(God the Father) has saved us and called us with a holy calling, (referring to God's Holy plan for our lives) not according to our works (plans), but **according to His own purpose** (plans) and **grace which was given to us** in Christ Jesus **before time began**.*

Boldly declare — *"I am a new creation person. I have a God-given destiny. **The grace I need to fulfill this plan of God was given to me before time began.**"*

> **Ephesians 2:10 (NIV)** *For we are God's workmanship, created in Christ Jesus **to do good works**, which **God prepared** in advance for us to do.*

Boldly declare — *"God has personally chosen me for an assignment that only I can fulfill. I am very important to the Father. **God has entrusted eternal souls into my care,** because He trusts me. Jesus will bring this to pass in my life. My faith is in Him to do it through me. I am not trusting in the flesh. I will reach every soul He has prepared for my arrival."*

> **Acts 17:26 (NIV)** *From one man he made every nation of men, that they should inhabit the whole*

> earth; and he (God) determined **the times set for them (when they should be born)** and the **exact places** where they should live.

Boldly declare — *"God determined that I would be born at such a time as this. God determined the exact place where I should live. God determined that I would attend my church, so I could be trained and prepared for the assignment He has for me."*

> **Ephesians 1:11 (NIV)** In Christ we were also chosen, having been predestined **according to the plan of God** who works out everything in conformity **with the purpose of his will**.

Boldly declare — *"Father thank you for keeping me in your perfect plan. Thank you for showing me what you want me to do for you, day by day."*

> **1 Corinthians 3:5 (NIV)** What, after all, is Apollos? And what is Paul? Only servants, through whom you came to believe - **as the Lord has assigned to each his task**.

Boldly declare — *"The Father has assigned to each his task. God has given me my task and I will fulfill it. Praise God."*

> **Ecclesiastes 6:10 (NLT)** Everything has already been decided. It was known long ago what each

person would be. **So there's no use arguing with God about your destiny**.

Boldly declare — *"The Heavenly Father has a wonderful plan for my life, a plan of fulfillment, joy, excitement, abundance, health, prosperity, wonderful times with my family, great friends, **as I extend His Kingdom and do my part to bring in the great harvest of lost souls, and strengthen other Christians**."*

"Everybody loves me; everybody wants to be around me, I flow in God's wisdom, love, peace, and joy. I am an encouragement to everybody. God's anointing heals the sick and drives out demons through me."

> **Jeremiah 29:11 (NIV)** *"For I know the plans I have for you," declares the Lord, "plans to prosper you and not to harm you, plans to give you hope and a future."*

Boldly declare — *"I believe Jeremiah 29:11 is true. My Heavenly Father loves me, and I am determined for other people to experience this love as well. This is who I am. I am a new creation. I am who God says I am. God sees me this way. He said all this about me; I am so excited to be what He sees me to be."*

The Father loves you children of God, you are His and He is yours. Enjoy your love relationship with your Loving Father.

Dr Theo Wolmarans

Conclusion

If you don't know the Lord Jesus Christ as Lord and Savior, please pray this:

Dear Father in Heaven,

Thank you for sending Jesus to die on a cross in my place. He died for the sins I committed. Lord Jesus, please forgive me for every sin I've ever committed. Thank you, and I forgive all those who have offended me. Come into my heart and save my life. I declare you are my Savior and You are my Lord. I will live for you with all of my heart until I see you face to face. Thank you for saving me. Because I've made Jesus my Lord and Savior, I'm bound for Heaven and God is my Father. Thank you for saving me, forgiving me and accepting me just as I am.

Amen.

Printed in the USA
CPSIA information can be obtained
at www.ICGtesting.com
LVHW021939271023
762359LV00045B/1052

9 780620 579520